Giggles in
the Garden

To Judy

"Keep the Corners
turned up!"

Phyllis
Gal 2:20

ISBN-13 978-1-60145-349-5
ISBN-10 1-60145-349-3

Printed in the United States of America.

Booklocker.com, Inc.
2007

All Scripture References are from the King James Version (KJV) and the New International Version (NIV) of the Holy Bible.

Edited by Brian and Jodie Spence

Dedication

Much love to our husbands, children, and grandchildren.
You are the flowers in our Gardens of Life.

Giggles in the Garden

Table of Contents

Introduction 1

Phyllis and I have been friends for over 25 years and have experienced a lot of life together. We attended the same church, and we laughed, loved, cried, served, comforted, praised, raised children, worked on projects, and worshipped together. We know each other pretty well! Some might say that's a *scary thing*. We are very thankful for these many years of life in each other's company.

Throughout the years we have learned that, regardless of our circumstances or situations, **God has always been faithful**. He has helped us maintain our balance and our sense of humor about life. We have giggled and laughed and enjoyed the ride.

Not long ago, I walked into Phyllis' kitchen and said to her, *"Phyllis, why don't you co-write a book with me?"*

She turned around and looked at me as if I were from outer space, slanted her eyes, and responded in a tight voice, *"Why did you ask me that?"*

It was not the answer I expected. I began to explain the type of book I had in mind. Not knowing what she was thinking, I quickly said, *"Well, just pray about it."*

It was not long before we had our two heads together, planning, and writing to put together this book. I found out that God had been telling Phyllis to write for quite some time. Having already written a couple of books, I know how it can be to take that first step and write those first lines.

We have had a wonderful time telling tales, remembering events, and writing stories about things that happened in our lives, the people in our lives, and situations that had an impact on our lives and on the lives of others.

We want you to have as much fun reading our antidotes as we had writing them. Everything in this book is true. We did not change any names, not even our own, to protect anybody. We just told the story the way it happened.

Our hearts' desire is to point others to God so that they will know the awesome joy that He brings. Yes, life does have problems, but it is the peace and love of our Savior that keeps us laughing.

God showers us with the giggles. It is contagious!

Come join us in the Garden!

With Love,

Linda Felker

Introduction 2

Ladies filled the garden with beauty and giggles. What a fun time we had. We were having a wedding shower brunch for my close friend. Ladies were wearing hats of all shapes and sizes and smiles to match. What a beautiful combination. It was a scene right out of *Southern Living Magazine*. There are events in our lives that should never come to an end. This was one of them.

My long-time friend, Linda, was in the garden that day and was inspired to ask me if I would co-author this book with her. I was flattered to say the least. Our first title was *Hats in the Garden*. The title soon changed to *Giggles in the Garden*. Why? Because as we were writing, we would giggle. We hope you will too. Fiction is exciting and sometimes funny, but nothing is better than truth. The stories in this book are from our lives: lives as big as two southern gals can live it!

With every new day, life holds possibilities that are new, fresh, and all just for you. God holds our lives in His hands. He knows our yesterday, today, and even our tomorrows. Why wouldn't we spend time with Him at the beginning of each new day since He knows what it holds for us?

I feel that if I give Him the first part of my day, everything just "fits" better. There are four ingredients to time spent with our Heavenly Father:

1. COFFEE – Coffee has to be first! I can't even find my socks or anything else until I've had my coffee!

2. BIBLE – Do not let anything take the place of spending time in God's Word. He wrote this book just for you. My pastor gave me a plan years ago that I try to follow. Proverbs has 31 chapters. Read a chapter for each day of the month. Some months, you'll have one extra!

3. PRAYER – Talking to the only One who can and will fix it, make it go away, heal it, change it, and if He doesn't, then give us peace about it! Whatever the "IT" is in our lives.

4. DEVOTIONAL BOOK – You need a feel-good book: *Giggles in the Garden.*

Keep the corners turned up!

Phyllis Spence

Life Giggles

Keep the Corners Turned Up

*"P*hyllis, why does your mouth look like this?"* My friend proceeded to show me what my mouth looked like.

I gasped! *"You have got to be kidding me. What do you mean my mouth looks like that?"*

She assured me that she was not kidding and that I needed to watch it! The corners of my mouth turned down and were headed as far south as they could possibly go without leaving my face.

It was not a pretty sight. Oh yes, and my lips were pooched out like a blowfish! I have no idea how long I had been doing that. I do believe it has something to do with the big five-O! I have heard all my life how things about your body seem to shift-move-drag-sag-migrate-disappear-get spotted-wrinkled-and just become overall disgustingly different.

I had no idea that my mouth was going to get involved in this metamorphosis, but it did. From that day to this, we have a sign that we use to help me. I told her to give me the sign when she saw me looking like that again, and I would immediately take care of it and turn up the corners.

As I was sitting beside my husband one Sunday in church, I looked over at him, and his mouth was in the same condition! It doesn't just affect women! Men can get it too! His corners were turned down, and his lips pooched out like there was not a muscle anywhere in his face working properly.

I gave him an elbow in the ribs! He looked up at me, and I was able to make him understand that he too had the "poochie lip" problem. He immediately turned the corners up and pulled in the lips. On our way home, we decided on a signal. If either of us saw the other with a mouth emergency, we would give the sign: a crooked index finger. The sign would be very discreet and hopefully, very effective. He and I have used the "sign" many times.

As I sit in the choir on Sunday and look out over the congregation, I see many people who could benefit from the "sign." I just cannot tell them one-on-one. I hope you will have a loved one or good friend like I did that will ask the question, *"Why do you look like this?"* If you look around in a congregation of people, you will see what I am talking about. For goodness sake, please help your friends (and ask them to discreetly help you).

Remember things are falling, and it's not stars! Be careful! I'm desperately trying to wipe out the "poochie lip" problem! They can't survive through a smile!

Now you know when I sign my name to a note with *"Keep the corners turned up,"* that I want to help somebody. I always hope someone will ask the question *"What does 'Keep the corners turned up' mean?"* I thought you'd never ask! Now you know: Keep the Corners Turned Up!

Proverbs 15:13
"A merry heart maketh a cheerful countenance: but by sorrow of the heart the spirit is broken." (KJV)

PS

Life Goes Better With Giggles

F ind something in your busy life today that makes you giggle. If you lay your head on your pillow tonight and have not had a reason to giggle, then you have missed something special.

Life is sometimes hard, and giggles make it easier. Just listen to a baby's laugh. It's not suppressed or full of anxiety. It's free, honest, and genuine. It's an honest-to-goodness giggle. If you have an opportunity to hear a baby giggle, you will likely smile. Listen as children play. Giggles will abound. Go to a swimming pool full of children. The screams and giggles will be contagious. Sit with your eyes closed and listen. The sounds are those of children just being children. Laughter is a very vital part of life.

I remember when Brian smiled the first time. I was singing "Jesus Loves Me" to him, and he smiled. One of our most precious treasures is a tape recording of Brian giggling, even before he could speak a word.

The first thing that impressed me about Brian's wife Jodie was her laugh! She has an honest-to-goodness, genuine, deep-down-inside laugh. You can trust people who know how to laugh. I trust Jodie. I gave her my son, and she is doing a great job being my daughter-in-law. I am looking forward to a lifetime of laughter with Brian and Jodie.

We are God's children so we have many reasons to rejoice and be happy. Our Heavenly Father created us and gave us the ability to laugh. He knows what today will hold for each of us. He tells us in His Word not to worry. A long time before the world coined the expression, *"Don't worry, be happy,"* God had already commanded us to do just that! He speaks often about joy, happiness, and rejoicing. Even when our circumstances don't call for joy, we can rejoice in Him, knowing that He has our lives in His control.

So go on and giggle. It's good for you!

Luke 12:22
"Then Jesus said to his disciples: 'Therefore I tell you, do not worry about your life, what you will eat; or about your body, what you will wear.'" (NIV)

John 16:33
"These things I have spoken unto you, that in me ye might have peace. In the world ye shall have tribulation; but be of good cheer; I have overcome the world." (KJV)

PS

Wear Your Hat to a Garden Party

When Brian and Jodie were engaged to be married, I planned to have a Garden Bridal Shower for Jodie. Everything was planned: beautiful round tables with white tablecloths to the ground. Every table was set with a different china pattern, thanks to friends like Anne and Donna. I even painted my wheelbarrow white and added ribbon and tulle to the handles.

Everything perfect? No! The weather was terrible, and the garden party turned into a "carport" party. It was just not the same. That was in 2003. Just this past spring in 2007, I had another opportunity to give a Garden Bridal Shower.

My friend Yurami is from Venezuela and had been living with us for six years. Yurami met and fell in love with David. Before they were married, I gave her a garden party. The invitations read:

Please join Yurami and her friends
in the garden
for a wedding shower brunch
at 11:00 until 2:00 in the afternoon
Ladies, let's have lots of fun - wear your hat

In my opinion, ladies don't have enough occasions to wear their hats.

Everything was going great. The garden was going to be perfect. I watched as everything in the garden bloomed in turn.

When the azaleas were just beginning to have their turn, a hard freeze came, and everything that was new "bit the dust." What a mess! Oh well, the party must go on. I bought a few new plants just to add a touch of color that the freeze had taken away.

As each lady came into the garden, they were giggling and having fun from the very start. There's just something about putting on a hat – it makes you smile. What fun we had that day in the garden with our hats on. If you want to have fun, put up some folding tables in the yard, throw on some tablecloths, invite some friends, and wear your hats. You will giggle, I promise. It doesn't matter what kind of food you serve or what you have planted in your garden.

The flowers walk into your garden under the hats. It has often been said, *"A garden of friends is always in full bloom."* I have heard nothing but *"Thank you,"* and *"What a blessing the shower was!"* from the guests.

I saw my friend Paula in church on Sunday after the shower, and she said, *"Phyllis, I have heard about garden parties all my life, but I've never been to one. I want to thank you for inviting me."* Paula is from the North. Don't you know that she had fun in the garden, southern style!

Some of our Lord's most wonderful and horrible moments came in the garden. Just hours after our garden party, a storm came, and it was bad. It started on Sunday evening right before leaving for church. Rain and hail coming down in buckets, and the buckets were full and running over! Speaking of buckets, I was running through the house trying to get pans to catch water because the hail was causing the roof to leak. The hail covered the garden. The plants that had survived the freeze were now beaten up by the hail.

On Monday morning, we had wind like I had never seen. We had 23 white pines that lined the backyard (the garden area). These trees were 45 years old and from 75 to 100 feet tall. One of them had already split. Being very alarmed, we called a tree man to come and look at it.

He said, *"There is nothing that I can do today. It is just too dangerous to put man or machine near these trees. This tree is going to fall today, and it will hit your house. Call me when it does, and I will come and put a tarp over your roof. And it's not safe for you to be standing in this room."*

He was speaking about my den. He also told me that the rest of the trees would probably continue to fall during the day. The first one fell, breaking off about 15 feet up. Because it broke so high above the ground, it only grazed the house, tearing off the gutter and slightly damaging the roof. Thank you, Lord!

My friend Blondell was watching the trees from the kitchen window when the first tree fell, and she called out to me, *"Phyllis, here it comes!"*

I was in the den and trying to run to the kitchen. I felt as though I was running in slow motion. We ran out of the house and stood outside when a second tree finally fell.

I waited for the rest of the day for the others to fall. They didn't. The two trees that fell grazed the house, but the damage wasn't as bad as it could have been. The first tree broke about 15 feet off the ground. The second one fell at an angle away from the house and avoided a direct hit to the roof.

The next day, we called a tree removal service that came and took down the remaining 21 trees.

My garden didn't look good anymore. Instead, it looked as though a bomb had exploded. I went into the garden with my hat on once again. But this time it was my work hat, and I started picking up broken limbs, birdhouses, bird feeders, potted plants, and broken lawn furniture. When you go to the garden, it doesn't matter if you have on your "party" hat or your "work" hat, the fellowship can be just as sweet.

I met God in the garden after the storm. He was still the same. My faith in Him after the storm is stronger than ever. Oh, what sweet fellowship can be had after the storm.

Nahum 1:3 and 7
"...the Lord hath his way in the whirlwind and in the storm, and the clouds are the dust of his feet...The Lord is good, a strong hold in the day of trouble; and he knoweth them that trust in him." (KJV)

PS

"I Can't Take My Jacket Off"

Iusually take a sweater with me to church during the spring and summer months. The air conditioning seems to go right through me, and I sit there with chill bumps running up and down my arms. It is normal for me to wrap up in a sweater at every service.

One Sunday morning, I forgot and left my sweater at home. Sitting next to my husband during preaching that day, I started shivering. There was no sweater to put around my shoulders, and I realized that I was going to have to deal with it unless I could find something else to wrap-up in.

I looked at my husband sitting next to me and had an idea. Leaning close to his ear, I whispered, *"Dave, please take off your suit jacket and give it to me. I'm so cold and need to wear it."*

My husband replied in a very low voice, *"Sorry, Babe, but I can't take off my jacket. I did not iron the back of my shirt."*

To compensate, he put his arm around my shoulder and drew me close up under his arm. His hand stroked my exposed arm throughout the entire service, trying to create warmth. The people sitting behind us probably had no idea why this man was being so cozy in the middle of a church service!

Our lives are the same as Dave's shirt. We iron the part that other people can see and show up for life looking crisp and fresh. However, the hidden part of our lives may not look too good.

When we are forced to take off the "jacket," our true self is exposed.

Wouldn't it be easier to iron the entire shirt in the first place?

Psalm 44:21
"...he knoweth the secrets of the heart." (KJV)

LF

French Fries and Seagulls

It was girls' weekend at Myrtle Beach, and we were having a ball. Two of my good friends and I drove to the beach early on a Friday morning and spent the next two days laughing and giggling as we did all the girl things that we love. We shopped, ate, had manicures and facials, and just enjoyed spending time together.

On our last morning there, we were up early so that we could spend time on the beach before the drive home. As we were leaving the room, one of my friends said, *"There are some leftover french fries in that bag. Let's take them with us and feed the birds."*

I did not really think that was a good idea but did not say anything. I just went along, and soon we were walking along the beach, enjoying the sea breeze.

There is nothing quite like the feeling of warm, wet sand between your toes. I wanted to spend more time walking than sitting under an umbrella. As my friends set up their chairs and kicked back for a little sun, I told them I was going to continue strolling on the beach.

I was reminded to take the bag of french fries and feed them to the seagulls that were hovering above us, and I agreed. Why I agreed, I do not know. I soon found out what a big mistake that was.

The first few fries I threw toward the seagulls were immediately snapped up in mid-air. I reached into the bag, grabbed the rest of the fries, pulled them out, and tossed them skyward. I noticed there seemed to be more birds flying around up there than had been there a moment before.

As I continued walking on the beach, I heard this *"hawking"* sound above me. I looked up and saw this great host of seagulls descending upon me. They were almost flying in formation towards me, and they started diving at the empty bag I was holding in my hand.

I started running, and the birds kept coming! That is when I discovered that, although warm, wet sand feels great between your toes when you are leisurely strolling on the beach, it is *terrible* when you are running from a flock of hungry birds!

But run I did! I just could not believe those birds were chasing me. My friends, who were observing this spectacle from their comfortable chairs, fell over laughing at me. I ran to them and then ran past them. I ran almost all the way to the pier before those seagulls gave up and left me alone. What a hilarious sight I must have been trying to out-run those birds.

Thinking back on it, I could have easily extricated myself from this situation if I had only thrown down the bag. They wanted my *"baggage,"* not me.

What "baggage" are you running with? Get rid of it! It weighs you down and makes you a target to the enemy.

I learned two lessons from this experience. First, never feed french fries to a seagull. Second, always wear tennis shoes when running on wet sand.

Hebrews 12:1

"Wherefore seeing we also are compassed about with so great a cloud of witnesses, let us lay aside every weight, and the sin which doth so easily beset us, and let us run with patience the race that is set before us." (KJV)

LF

My Priceless Treasure

A mother is a priceless treasure that money cannot buy. When we are separated from our treasure, our hearts are sad.

Where do I begin to tell you about my mother's home-going to heaven? I say "home-going" because the word "death" is just too painfully hard. Southerners have a way of making the hardest words softer, more pleasant if you would.

My mom was a tough, southern-to-the-bone gal. She not only had a southern accent, she had a language all her own! A lady from Venezuela came to live with my parents while she was preparing for school here in the United States. She wanted to live with an American family in order to learn English faster. We laughed that Mom would be her tutor. She would not only be learning English, she would be learning "Mom!"

In Mom's language, "clem" meant to climb, "nare" meant narrow, "roastees" meant two or more roasts, and "salit" meant salad. I could go on and on. We loved her words, and we laughed with her, never at her. Mom loved to laugh.

Mom had suffered through two broken hips, a heart attack, a stroke, a broken arm, a broken wrist, a broken foot, a broken pelvis, and cancer. Now you tell me, was she tough or what?

One morning she got out of bed, went to the bathroom, and then walked into the den. She sat down on the sofa and told Dad to come sit down beside her. She laughed because he was wearing her glasses by mistake. Then she fell over on the sofa unconscious.

As the ambulance rushed her to the hospital, I expected her to pull through, just as she had so many times before. This time, however, it was not to be. She never regained consciousness. Instead, she went home to heaven.

Did you notice that the last sound she made on this earth was to laugh? Ladies always know when it is time to leave, and my mom was such a lady. I sat on her bedside and held and kissed her beautiful hands as she left me. After she left, I got busy making all the necessary arrangements.

The one thing I thought my heart could not endure was to look at my mom in a casket. However, I did it. It wasn't easy, but I did it. She was beautiful. Her dress was gorgeous, the most awesome Easter dress she had ever owned. Did I tell you that she went home on Good Friday? Visitation was on Easter Sunday evening, and she was buried in her church cemetery on Easter Monday. What an Easter.

The word "buried" comes a little easier to me now because of a seven-year-old boy named Gilson. He sings in my children's choir at church. His "out-of-the-mouth-of-babes" statement has given me a word picture to carry in my heart about my mom's death.

Gilson and his mother came to my mom's viewing and gave me a much-needed hug. His mother told me that when he saw my mom, he said, *"Oh look, she is asleep in the treasure chest."*

Wow! That was just what I needed to hear. Yes, Gilson, she is asleep, and that beautiful lady is buried only for a little while.

It will not be long before I will be reunited with my treasure: my mom. I will ever be thankful to this blonde-haired, "adult-thinking" little boy who let me see my mom's home-going through the eyes of a child. She was my treasure, and I have buried her for only a little while. She truly is *"asleep in the treasure chest."*

1 Thessalonians 4:14
"We believe that Jesus died and rose again and so we believe that God will bring with Jesus those who have fallen asleep in him." (NIV)

PS

Dodgeball

I do not like the game of Dodgeball. There are several reasons why this game bothers me. First, I do not like to be a target. Standing in the middle of a circle and allowing other people to throw a large, hard ball at me is not my idea of having fun.

Second, I do not like being hit. Just when I think I have maneuvered myself to a position of safety, I get hit smack in the back of the head. It is usually not a soft hit but a whopping, resounding, powerful blow. It hurts.

Third, I do not like being thrown out of the game when I get hit by the ball. Having to walk out of the circle in front of everyone, acknowledging that I was not clever enough, fast enough, or smart enough to avoid the ball is humiliating.

Lastly, I do not like sitting on the sidelines while everyone else is still playing. Watching them laugh and run while I sit brooding outside the circle makes me feel ignored, embarrassed, and left out.

Life is like Dodgeball. Just when you think you have managed to avoid being hit by the ball, something clobbers you in the back of the head. You are taken by surprise and go limping to the sidelines of life, totally unaware that the ball was even in the court!

Once benched, there are several reactions you might take. You might cry and feel sorry for yourself. As you sit there, human nature might take over, and feelings of hurt, disappointment, or even anger emerge.

Why did this happen to me? I was doing my best to avoid the ball, weaving, and running, trying to keep up with life, trying to live right, and do right. Then suddenly, **BAM**, right upside the head. Surely, I did not deserve this to happen to me.

Or you might look around and start comparing yourself to others who are still in the game. Why not them? They are not living right, making all kinds of blunders, yet they are still in the game. Nothing bad ever seems to happen to those people.

My mother always said that some people have to learn everything the hard way. She was so right, and at times, I have been just that way. Instead of making an effort to learn something positive in those difficult moments of life, I have wallowed around in self-pity and emotional distress.

If you are a Christian, you will always be a target to the enemy. The best reaction when you are hit by the ball is to learn whatever lesson there is to learn from the experience, be thankful for the opportunity to play, and then get back in the game as fast as you can.

If you sit back and feel sorry for yourself, you may never overcome the situation.

Usually, the best life lessons can be learned when you are sitting on the bench.

Psalm 60:12
"With God we will gain the victory..." (NIV)

1 Corinthians 15:57
"But thanks be to God, which giveth us the victory through our Lord Jesus Christ." (KJV)

LF

Twilight Time

My father, orphaned when he was a young boy, grew up in the post-depression era by being passed from relative to relative. Not having a real home with loving parents was hard for this lonely young boy, but he learned to protect himself and survived his childhood living on handouts and hand-me-downs.

These experiences instilled in him the need to be in control, protect his belongings, and have a home and family of his own. He met my mother when she was 15 years old and immediately knew that this cute little redhead was the woman he would love forever.

After serving in the Army during World War II, stationed in Germany, he returned to the United States and married my mother. Life was not easy for this young couple, but they lived and raised four children together. My father finally had the family he had always longed for.

As we were growing up, he often told us stories of his growing-up years, and I could see the pain behind those clear blue eyes and imagine the struggles he must have encountered as a poverty-stricken orphan trying to survive alone.

He told the story of evening time when he was young and how he wondered where he was going to sleep for the night. The nighttime hours were the most difficult, and he was often scared, hungry, and alone.

I can remember his booming voice calling all of us children home at the end of the day. He would stand in the front yard and call us by name, *"Sue, Linda, Clark, Joey, come on in the house. It's getting dark."* It was twilight time, and he made sure all his children were inside. We never experienced the fear of not having a home.

My father had a powerful singing voice and sang in a Southern Gospel Quartet for most of his adult life. He was the choir director at our church, and there was nothing he loved more than singing. As he grew older, his voice began to waver and crack, but that did not stop him from trying to sing the songs that he loved best.

23

Two years ago, I sat by my father's bedside as he lay in a coma. The doctors told us that there was nothing more they could do for him and that he would probably leave us within a few days.

His blue eyes were closed; his breathing seemed labored and uneasy. I wondered what was going on behind those closed eyes. Could he hear us when we talked to him? What was he thinking? I asked his nurses, but they could only assure me that he was not in pain, for which we were all thankful.

Sitting there, I talked to my dad, hoping for some reaction so that I would know he heard what I was saying. I needed him to understand that he was not alone. He had been alone in this world for all those early years of his life; I wanted him to know he was not alone going out.

Nothing my mother said, or I said, or any of the other many family members said, brought any response from Daddy. My heart was heavy, wanting to reach my father one last time and tell him things that were on my heart.

Then my mother said, *"Linda, sing to him."* I thought about it for a moment, then stood up, and leaned down close to my father's ear. I began to sing to my father in a low voice, only loud enough for him to hear.

I felt a calm spirit wash over me, and my voice became louder and clearer. I sang "Where the Roses Never Fade," a song that he and I had sung together many times. I sang other songs about heaven, and I sang "Amazing Grace."

Looking down at my father's face, his eyes still closed and body unmoving, I noticed tears rolling down his cheeks. I am convinced he heard me. I had connected with him at last.

At 7 p.m. that evening, my father went home to heaven. That night, God stepped outside His house and called my father's name. *"Joe Fox, it's time to come on in the house."*

I am so thankful for those moments I had with him, singing to him, and seeing those tears trickle from his eyes. My father was a Christian, and God had always been there, keeping him safe, and meeting his needs.

Regardless of your situation, remember that God loves you. He will never leave you or forsake you. Though the world may be unkind, there is always refuge in the Lord. My father knew this, and I rejoice in the knowledge that he is now in his permanent home in heaven.

Psalm 116:15
"Precious in the sight of the Lord is the death of his saints." (KJV)

LF

"I Left His Head Out"

It isn't unusual for birds to fly into our glass patio doors, thinking it is a thoroughfare. One day I was on house-cleaning duty, which caused me to pass by the glass doors several times. On one of my passes, I noticed a bird had tried to fly through the glass and had knocked himself out.

My son Brian and his friend Christy, both of whom were still too young to go to school, came charging into the house. They had found their mission for the day. They were going to revive the injured bird. Poor little fellow! And he thought things were bad when he conked himself in the head with a hard, invisible door. Now he was on the ground, helpless, and trapped in his motionless, ruffled, feathered body! You would think that it just couldn't get any worse for the little fellow. It could, and it did.

Brian and Christy set out on their mission of mercy with water, crackers, bread, little dishes, pine straw, little bandages, and whatever else they thought that a knocked-out bird might need to survive. I passed the door several more times during my cleaning duty, which I hated almost as bad as the bird hated his predicament.

There were the three of them: with two working together as a team on a mission of mercy and one as a "victim." The bird just sat there nodding his little head, surrounded with little dishes of water and breadcrumbs, being ministered to by the young ER trauma team.

What could be worse than flying full-speed, head-first into a glass door? Try this! *Flying full-speed, head-first into a glass door and then being force-fed bread and water by two small, unsophisticated, untrained but self-appointed healthcare workers when you are unable to move any part of your body, except for an occasional head-nod while you are desperately trying to escape your unwanted assistants!*

Well, what do you know? On one of my cleaning passes, the bird was gone. All that was left behind were little dishes of bread and water. Yea, he made it! Despite all of the odds to the contrary, I concluded that the medical team had completed their mission and that the bird had recovered! When Brian and Christy came into the house, I congratulated them on a job well done.

Brian quickly responded, *"No, Mom, he died."*

"Oh, how sad," I replied. My sadness immediately turned to "get-out-of-the-room-fast and don't let them see you laughing!"

Brian explained, *"We buried him in the garden, but we left his head sticking out so no one would step on him."*

You see now why I had to get out of the room as fast as possible. Can you picture that poor bird in your mind's eye? I surely did, and it was a sight! Brian, you are in full charge of *my* burial! I like the way this child thinks!

Proverbs 20:11
"Even a child is known by his doings, whether his work be pure, and whether it be right." (KJV)

PS

Prayer Giggles

Swimming at Dawn

There were two things I was afraid of as a child; water was one of them, and heights was another. While the other children were splashing around in the community swimming pool, I was sitting on the side watching them have fun.

I carried these fears with me into adulthood and did my best to avoid those situations. However, after my children were born, my inability to swim became a sore spot, and I was determined that they would not grow up with the burden of not being able to swim.

I enrolled them in swimming lessons, and by the time they were three years old, both of them could swim quite well. They had no fear of the water and certainly no fear of heights as they jumped into the deep end of the pool.

Marci and Todd could jump off the diving board, turn flips in the air, hit the water hard, and come up laughing! They amazed me, and I was so glad that they did not have this same fear that had paralyzed me all my life.

One year on vacation at the beach, as I sat on the sidelines watching my two children take running starts and jump headfirst into the deep end of the pool, I became quite concerned. I was a mother, and mothers need to be able to protect their children.

What if one of my kids got hurt in the pool? What if they got in trouble in the water and needed my help? What if one of them hit their head on the bottom of the pool? What if...?

I realized that it was my motherly duty to learn to swim and overcome my fear of water. The very idea of it was scary, but I knew I had to do it for them!

Naturally, I did not want my children to know that they could do something I could not do. I had managed to keep it from them, and they did not know about my fear of the water. I had always told them I did not want to get my hair wet or would rather just watch them than actually get into the pool with them.

I was in a dilemma. How could I learn to swim without drawing too much attention to myself? I came up with an answer and decided what I would do.

Early the next morning just after the sun came up, I suited up and headed for the pool. As my family lay sleeping, as the entire complex lay sleeping, I stood at the edge of the swimming pool and looked at the water.

"OK, Linda, this is your chance. Go ahead – jump in," I said to mentally prepare myself. Positioning myself at the end of the eight-foot deep end of the pool, I closed my eyes, took a deep breath, and jumped in the water.

Now I ask you, *how stupid was that*? There was not another soul around. It was 6 o'clock in the morning! I hit the water hard and went straight to the bottom of the pool. Sputtering and gasping, I fought my way back to the top, and down I went again.

I started fighting the water, beating it with my hands and flailing my legs, trying to stay on top. Somehow, I managed to get back to the side of the pool and grasped hold of the slippery concrete with both arms. I was hanging half in and half out of the water.

What do I do now? I could not get out, and I certainly did not want to go back in. I was surely stuck. Calling for help would do no good; there was no one around to hear me.

"Oh, Lord! It's me again, and I'm in trouble. Help me!" I prayed aloud with my eyes open and hanging on for dear life.

Logic told me to hang onto the side, work my way toward the shallow end of the pool, and climb out the steps. However, stubbornness won out over logic, and my determination took over. I let go of my grip on the slippery side of the pool and pushed myself back into the water.

For two hours, I forced myself to stay in that eight-foot water. I refused to give up or give in. I kept at it until I was able to move from one side of the pool to the other without swallowing too much chlorine.

Then, I wanted a cup of coffee! Emerging from the water, I crept back into the room to find my family still sleeping. I filled my coffee cup and went back outside. Sitting in a lounge chair in the garden beside the pool, I began to think about the risky thing I had done.

I could have died in that water! I took an extreme chance by diving in with no obvious means of rescue if I failed.

Later that day, my children were once again jumping off the diving board and playing Marco Polo. I swam up beside them and joined in the fun! They were just glad I was there. So was I!

Have you ever jumped in over your head? Against all common sense and reason, did you dive into something dangerous? Even though you knew you were making a big mistake, did you plunge forward anyway?

Sometimes we make foolish, irrational decisions and find ourselves hanging onto the side trying to figure out how to survive. Being the human being that I am, there have been many times when I have jumped into a situation that was over my head. Without a life vest, without a visible means of escape, I plunged right in to the deep water.

I am convinced that God has a great sense of humor. Just picture how ridiculous I must have looked, soaking wet, gasping, and hanging onto the side of the pool, a 32-year-old woman who jumped into the water and did not know how to swim.

God must have been lovingly laughing aloud as He not only saved me from drowning but also helped me learn to swim.

God was my Lifeguard that morning. He still is.

Psalm 25:20
"Guard my life and rescue me; let me not be put to shame, for I take refuge in you." (NIV)

LF

The Class Ring

W hen I was in high school, my class ring cost about $59.00. Our son Brian came home from school and announced that his class ring was going to cost in the neighborhood of $300.00!

So you can only imagine how upset I was later when Brian made another announcement just as shocking: *"Mom, I've lost my class ring."*

I told him, *"For right now, don't tell the 'daddy person' that you lost your ring."* Some news needs to wait just a little while before being shared with him. Who knows, we might just find it. Why should all three of us be upset?

The ring was missing for several months. During that time, his dad didn't notice one time that it was gone. Brian would go on "big class ring hunts" every now and then.

One day I was cooking dinner when I noticed that he had turned over the recliner and was throwing sofa pillows left and right. Then he headed for his car and came back into the kitchen with bags of fast food trash and junk.

I said, *"Brian, what are you doing?"*

He said, *"Mom, I really do want to find my class ring."* I began thinking that there must be a girl in the picture; we would see.

All of a sudden, this came from my mouth: *"Brian, have you asked the Lord to help you find your ring? You know whatever is important to us is important to Him."*

He replied in that *"Whatever, Mom"* tone of voice that teens can throw out in a second, *"No, Mom, I haven't."*

I said, *"Brian, go to a private place and just ask the Lord to help you, and as you pray, I will be praying as I work."*

Reluctantly, he did just that. He was willing to try anything at this point. I turned back to my work. I was whipping up something, and boy, did it get whipped double time.

I started talking to the Lord, *"Now Lord, you know how teenagers are; they think moms and dads who talk to You about lost class rings and the like are a little shy of a full load. If You will ever answer a prayer for me, let it be now. I have two reasons for really wanting an answer. First, we need to find this ring before the 'daddy person' finds out that it's missing, and second, I really want Brian to know that prayer works."*

So there I was in the kitchen, praying like never before. I was on a mission. *"Please Lord, Please!"* I finished my work in the kitchen, and as I waited on my husband to come home from work, I went into the living room to relax and play the piano. I needed to forget all about the "great class ring hunt" for the moment.

In a few minutes, Brian came into the room with his hands behind his back. He said, *"Mom."*

I thought to myself, *"What does this kid need now?"* I certainly wasn't expecting news on the class ring this fast. He wasn't going to go away so I looked up from the piano to see what he wanted.

There he stood, hand extended, showing off the most beautiful class ring I'd ever seen in my life. He was giving a standing ovation performance of Fred Sanford's rendition of "If I Didn't Care"! We started jumping, laughing, and telling the Lord, *"thank you, thank you, thank you!"*

Brian didn't think that prayer would work at all, and I really didn't think it would work that fast! Boy, did God prove us both wrong! How glad we are when God answers our prayers, especially when we really have a lot of self-doubt.

I guess you would like to know where the class ring was? He had looked downstairs in a closet of outgrown clothes destined for the thrift shop. The ring was in the pocket of a pair of pants that he had outgrown. Now I wonder why he ever thought to look there? I think I know the answer.

Philippians 4:6
"Be careful for nothing; but in every thing by prayer and supplication with thanksgiving let your requests be made known unto God." (KJV)

PS

Singing the Blessing

There is nothing more touching than the sincere prayer of a child. It is pure, simple, innocent, and completely trusting. There are no big words, no pretense, and no attempt to impress anyone.

A child prays as if he is snuggled up in God's lap and whispering in His ear, and the child fully expects God to answer his prayer right then. They have no doubts, and there are no half-hearted attempts to connect with God. A child prays in a straightforward manner, using powerful little words to reach the heart of God.

In the First Grade Sunday School Class one morning, it was my grandson Zachary's turn to lead in prayer. The teacher had asked for prayer requests, and each child around the table told of something they wanted or needed. There were no huge "adult-like" requests, just one-line statements from each child.

Zachary bowed his head on the table and launched into prayer. His prayer began with, *"Hey Lord, see that girl over there in the blue dress? She skinned her knee. Please make it better."* Zachary pointed his hand toward the little girl across the table wearing the blue dress, making sure God knew exactly which one he was talking about.

He continued to pray aloud, talking to God as if He were standing right next to him.

Priceless! That child had no doubt in his mind whatsoever that God would immediately heal that skinned knee. He prayed with complete trust and expectation. He prayed with faith.

How many times do you pray with complete faith and trust? Do you pray believing the answer is on the way, or is there a portion of your heart and mind that harbors doubt? Where is your faith when you pray?

Matthew 17:20
"...If ye have faith as a grain of mustard seed...nothing shall be impossible unto you." (KJV)

After church that Sunday, my family gathered around my dining room table for lunch. Zachary, six years old, and Jackson, three years old, always say the blessing. But they do not "speak" it; they sing it!

To the tune of the children's song, "Are You Sleeping Brother John," they sing these words: *"God Our Father, God Our Father, we thank You. We thank You. We thank you for our blessings. We thank you for our blessings. Amen. Amen."*

In fact, these boys "sing the blessing" every time they eat. It does not matter if they are in a restaurant or at home. They loudly sing the blessing!

How willing would you be to "sing the blessing" in the middle of a crowded restaurant? Would you be ashamed or embarrassed to bow your head and burst into song?

That Sunday, while the boys were singing the blessing, I bowed my head, pointed my hand toward Zachary and Jackson, and started to pray. *"God, see those boys sitting across the table? I pray they will always be willing to sing the blessing."*

James 1:6
"But let him ask in faith, nothing wavering…" (KJV)

LF

Safe in the Storm

For days, the weather forecast advised of a tropical storm that was moving up the east coast. At some point, the storm was upgraded to a hurricane, and residents were told to find safe shelter.

Hurricanes are especially dangerous to people who live in mobile homes. That was me. I lived in a trailer like many other *"Marine Corps Wives"* whose spouses were stationed at the Cherry Point Air Station near Morehead City, North Carolina. The base was about 30 miles away.

My baby Todd was a precious little bundle and at three months old, only weighed six pounds. Being born prematurely, it was a miracle he had survived. After many weeks in the intensive care nursery, we were finally allowed to bring him home from the military hospital.

I literally hovered over that child day and night. If he moved, I was there. If he hiccupped, I was there. I set my alarm clock to wake myself up every two hours so that I could feed the baby. Premature babies sleep all the time, and I was determined that, Lord willing, this child would grow and thrive.

That night, alone in the trailer with my baby, and a hurricane ripping up the coast, I was terrified. I looked out the windows, but could not see another person around. The sound of the rain beating down on the metal trailer was horrendous, and the wind of the approaching storm was already bending the pine trees to the ground.

A trailer is not a safe place to be in a hurricane. But I knew it would be worse to leave and try to make my way to the base. I took a heavy quilt, wrapped my baby and myself up as tight as I could, and sat down in the narrow hallway of the trailer. I pushed both my legs against one wall and my back against the other, wedging myself in, and cradling the baby against my chest.

"Oh, Lord, give me strength, and help me. God, protect us," I prayed over and over, continually, without ceasing.

The power went off around midnight and pitched us into total darkness. There were no lights inside the trailer, no streetlights outside. A few minutes later, what felt like the full force of the hurricane hit.

The trailer was rocking back and forth, blown by the tremendous winds. Water sprayed in through every crack in that metal box, and I pulled the quilt up over my head and braced my body for the blow I expected was coming.

"Oh, God, protect us!" I prayed as I forced my body to remain tightly wedged in the hallway.

After what seemed like hours, but was actually only a short time, the trailer stopped rocking. There was silence and darkness. Cautiously, I stood up and moved to the window. Amazed, I could see that the trailer was somehow in the same position as always, the rain was letting up, and the wind was subsiding. I unwrapped the quilt and saw that my son was still sleeping soundly. Precious child, wrapped up in his mother's arms, he had slept through the entire ordeal!

Later that day, I watched the news and saw pictures of the devastation in the surrounding community. But the trailer park where we lived was left untouched.

Oh, how thankful I am for God's protective hand. He surely protected us that night through the storm.

Psalm 56:3
"What time I am afraid, I will trust in thee." (KJV)

LF

Family Devotion Break Up

PJ's on and Bibles in hand, we headed to the sitting room for family devotion: my husband Guy, our son Brian, his friend Josh, and me. "Sitting room" sounds so Southern, doesn't it? At one time, our sitting room was a screened-in porch with one entrance from the den and another from our bedroom. The row of white pines behind our house made the porch impossible to enjoy because they kept everything dusty with their pollen all summer long. Finally, we closed it in, and what do you know: a sitting room. It was complete with prissy, pink wicker furniture. It was also cozy, inviting, and just right for family devotions.

Our family tried hard to make these family devotions a routine way of life. We would come together at the end of the day, our Bibles in hand, and our hearts turned to thoughts of our loving Heavenly Father.

I would like to tell you that we did this every night of our lives, but I can't say that. Life is so busy, and Satan is so real. The last thing he wants you to do is to have family time around God's Word. If he can cause a family any trouble, it will happen just when they are about to have family devotion. The phone rings, the cat throws up, the kids are fighting, the commode runs over, the power goes out, and oh yes, don't forget the doorbell. It will surely ring. You get the picture. I'm sure we've all been there, done that. Even though your devotion time with your family will not always be perfect, never give up or give in to failure. Once in a while is better than not at all.

So Josh was like family. He had been one of Brian's life-long friends. Oh, did these boys have some adventures. Once when Josh was spending the night with Brian, I called the boys into the sitting room for family devotion just before bedtime. They were about five years old. We explained to Josh that we would have devotion together before going to bed. Guy would read from the Bible, we would discuss what he had read, and then we would each pray in turn. Josh was told he did not have to pray if he didn't want to, but he said that he would.

41

After the Bible was read and discussions were finished, I prayed. Then Guy prayed, followed by Brian, and finally Josh.

Josh started with all the norms: *"God, bless Mom and Dad,"* and then he thanked Him for His blessings. Finally, he made a request that made us all open our eyes and drop our jaws: *"Lord, please help my dog climb a tree like a cat!"*

Devotion over, amen, go to bed, goodnight, sweet dreams, and see you in the morning! I had to keep talking!

When the boys were out of the room, Guy and I broke into uncontrollable laughter. We still laugh today when we think about the time our family devotion broke up into uncontrollable laughter. I believe there are times when God laughs—this just had to be one of those times.

Josh's request seemed ridiculous to us, childlike innocence. Didn't he know that dogs can't climb trees, that this was an impossible request? He definitely did not. And guess what? God didn't find it impossible either.

I don't know if Josh's dog ever climbed a tree like a cat. But sometimes when I feel like the request I am making of God is impossible, I like to picture that dog at the top of a tall tree looking down and thinking, *"Go ahead. Just ask."*

Got any dogs that need to climb a tree?

Matthew 21:21-22
"Jesus replied, 'I tell you the truth, if you have faith and do not doubt, not only can you do what was done to the fig tree, but also you can say to this mountain, "Go, throw yourself into the sea," and it will be done. If you believe, you will receive whatever you ask for in prayer.'" (NIV)

PS

Love Giggles

Kitty Banks

On a cool, crisp October day, my mother bundled up her three children, ages five, three, and two, and took us downtown to visit the First National Bank. She told us that when we got to the bank, a nice lady would give us a Kitty Bank.

The Kitty Bank was shaped like a cat, made of cardboard, and opened up like a greeting card. Inside, there were slots cut into the cardboard to put dimes. When all the slots were full, there would be $5.00 in the Kitty Bank.

The purpose of the Kitty Bank was to encourage children to save their dimes and use that money to open their own savings account. But my mother had a different purpose in mind.

Arriving at the bank, she paraded us through the lobby to the Savings Department. There were special wooden steps placed in front of the teller's window especially for children to use, and she placed us in a row on those steps in front of the smiling woman behind the counter.

The teller gave each of us a Kitty Bank and showed us how to put our dimes into the slots on the inside of the card. To get us started on our saving project, the teller put one dime into each of our cards.

On the way home, Mother explained what we were going to do with these little cardboard dime-savers. She said, *"Children, it is important that you learn to save your money. But you are not going to save your money to buy toys or candy. You are saving your dimes for Jesus' birthday."*

Mother said she would give us chores to do, so that we could earn dimes for our Kitty Banks. When the Kitty Banks were full, we would each have saved $5.00, and we could give the money to Jesus for a birthday present.

Mother wanted to make sure we understood the concept of saving. More importantly, she wanted to teach us the principle of giving back to

God a portion of what He had given us. She wanted us to experience the joy and excitement of being able to give.

One Sunday morning just before Christmas, we took our filled Kitty Banks to church. When the offering plate was passed, we carefully placed our banks into the plate. We did it with happy hearts and were glad to give to Jesus.

I would never have experienced this joy if my mother had not taken time to teach the lesson. Naturally, it would have been much easier for her to give us a little money to put in the offering plate. However, we would never have learned the valuable lesson of giving if she had done that.

What lessons are you teaching? There are so many opportunities to be an example for others, especially children. They are watching you and learning from your actions.

Matthew 10:8
"...Freely you have received, freely give." (NIV)

LF

The Christmas Closet

My parents had four children within six years! Naturally, with four children in the house and a multitude of grandparents, aunts, uncles, and various other relatives, there was an abundance of gifts at Christmas.

Going to my grandparents' house on Christmas Day was a tradition I looked forward to, knowing I would receive all those presents!

We would arrive by noon, and soon the house would be filled with the glorious aroma of turkey and spicy pumpkin pies. The children were all hyperactive, knowing that after the meal, we would go into the living room and begin opening the gifts.

At the end of the day, my weary parents would drive home in a car laden down with tired children, a trunk full of new toys, and of course, leftovers.

The next day, Mother would gather and sort through all the gifts we had received and try to figure out where to put all the stuff! We lived in a four-room house, with one bedroom for the four children and one bedroom for my parents.

There was a large closet in the hallway between the two bedrooms, and at the top of the closet was a storage area. Mother would select two gifts per child that we could keep and play with. All the others she stored in the top of the closet. Throughout the year, Mother would allow us to select a new toy from the box at the top of the closet.

There was a specific purpose in not allowing us to have all those toys at once. We were young and not able to understand the significance of the gifts. People were kind and generous to us, and even though we said, *"Thank you,"* we did not really comprehend that these gifts were not an entitlement but gifts from the heart.

She did not want us to think that Christmas was all about gifts and receiving a lot of "stuff." She taught us the true meaning of Christmas and about the birth of Jesus Christ. His birth represents the greatest gift of all!

Mother taught us the story of Jesus and made sure that we had a "head knowledge" long before we experienced the "heart knowledge." She planted a garden of knowledge into her children beginning during the young years, which prepared us to accept Christ when we were older.

Lastly, she wanted us to know that "things" would never really satisfy us. Toys break, dolls become dirty, and the shiny new tricycle will rust if left out in the yard.

God's great gift to us is everlasting. His love never changes, breaks, gets dirty, or rusts. It remains brand new forever.

My mother tended her "garden" of children carefully. She seeded her garden with stories of Jesus. She nurtured each budding child and gently formed each one with careful pruning, plenty of nourishment, a lot of discipline, and unconditional love.

What seeds are you planting in your garden? The tender heart of a child is rich soil in which to grow a garden that will honor and glorify God.

Hosea 10:12
"Sow for yourselves righteousness, reap the fruit of unfailing love..." (NIV)

LF

Mercy Found Me on the Curb

Thursday morning, a few days after I turned 17 years old, my father took me to the driver license office to take the driver's test. I had studied, completed the training, and I was ready. I easily passed the road test, written test, and eye test and was so proud to have my very own driver license.

Seventeen years old, brand new driver license in my hand, I was ready to roll! The only problem was that there was nothing for me to drive. Although I had a job working at the Buckaroo Steak House as a salad girl, I did not have enough money saved for a car, and my parents only had one car that they shared.

Two days later on Saturday morning, I asked my father if I could borrow his car to go to Hinkle's bookstore in Parkway Plaza Shopping Center, which was less than two miles from our house. I told him I needed to pick up some school supplies.

As he handed me the keys to his '67 Pontiac Tempest, he said, *"Go straight there, and come straight back."*

I said, *"OK,"* and flew out the door. My brother Clark was with me, and we jumped into the car and drove away from the house.

My first stop was several miles away at my best friend Vanessa's house. I pulled up in her driveway, and she came running out and got in the car. *"Let's go and pick up Patty, and then we can go to McDonald's for lunch,"* she said.

Away we went, driving across town to Patty's house. She got in the car, and now there were four of us. I backed down the driveway, across the street, and stopped at the curbside to change gears, when **WHAM**; a car came over the hill and slammed into the back of my daddy's only car.

Stunned, we scrambled out of the car. The lady who was driving the other vehicle jumped out and started screaming at me. *"Why were you parked on the side of the road? I could not see you when I came up over the hill! This is all your fault."*

The words *"All Your Fault"* rang in my ears, repeating over and over until I thought I would go crazy. Oh, No! My father! What would he say when he realized I had wrecked his only car.

The police arrived, and somebody got in touch with my parents and offered to give them a ride to the scene. Clark, Vanessa, and Patty were standing in the road beside the wrecked cars; I was sitting on the curb hysterically crying.

The police officer listened as the woman told her version of the story; then he wrote me a ticket, blaming me for the wreck. He never asked me any questions or gave me an opportunity to tell my side of the story. Instead, he walked over to me, handed me the ticket, and muttered, *"Stupid teenage drivers."*

About that time, my father arrived, and I was so afraid. I saw him talking to the police officers; I saw him talking to Clark; and finally, I saw him coming toward me. He did not say a word but reached down his hand and lifted me up off the curb. Putting his arm around me, he walked me to the car that drove us home.

Once back home, my father phoned the insurance company to notify them of the accident. Then, he went about his business as if nothing had happened.

I kept waiting for the worst. I expected some kind of punishment or at least for him to fuss at me for disobeying him. Remember, he had told me to go straight to the store, and come straight home. I did not do that. I drove all over town, and as a result of my disobedience, my father's car was totaled.

But my father never talked to me about the accident; he never accused me or made me feel bad. He knew I was at my lowest point right then and that I already knew what a big mistake I had made.

My father showed mercy for me when I least expected or deserved it. He withheld his anger and judgment from me. He never spoke of it again.

I learned years later that my father defended me to the police officer that day and took my side. He interceded for me and told the officer he was wrong for not allowing me to speak. Thankfully, the ticket was also dismissed.

What an example of God's love. Our Heavenly Father reaches down His hands and lifts us up off the curb of life. He extends mercy and forgiveness and casts our sins away, never to be remembered against us again.

Psalm 86:5
"For thou, Lord, art good, and ready to forgive; and plenteous in mercy unto all them that call upon thee." (KJV)

LF

A Present for Mommy

Todd loved to explore, and although I made sure he was contained inside a fenced yard, he could still investigate every corner, every tree, every dirt pile, every overhanging branch from the neighbor's yard, every square inch of yard we owned.

As I stood in the kitchen one summer morning washing the breakfast dishes, I heard Todd's sweet little voice calling me from the front door. *"Mommy, look what I found for you!"*

I thought to myself that he must have picked a flower from the garden as he usually did every day. The few blooms in my garden did not last very long. Todd always picked them as soon as they arrived and presented them to me with a big smile on his face. Then, they would go into a glass full of water and sit on the table during supper.

"I'll be right there," I said as I dried my hands and walked through the living room to the front door. I looked through the screen door, and there stood my child with a huge happy grin on his face, both arms extended, and his hands tightly holding what appeared to be a dead rat!

I screamed, dropped my dishtowel, and ran wildly toward the door. My four-year-old son stood there holding that dead "thing" out in front of him as a gift to me! He was so proud of bringing me this present!

I shouted, *"Throw it – throw it now."* Startled, Todd turned sideways and threw the dead "rat" off the porch. It landed on my front sidewalk in plain view for all to see.

"I found you a present, Mommy," my little boy said. *"Don't you want it?"*

Clearly, this child needed instruction on the proper little surprises to bring his mommy. I felt sick! Jerking the screen door open, I grabbed those little arms and hauled Todd straight into the house, down the hall, and into the bathroom. I ran a bathtub full of water and deposited my child into it in a hurry.

Pulling my long hair up into a ponytail and armed with soap and a washcloth, the scrubbing began. I scrubbed him from the top of his little head to the soles of his feet. Rinse – scrub again. I washed that child until his skin was glowing pink. All the while, he was twisting and turning, trying to get out of the tub. It was a proper battle! Who ever heard of taking a bath in the middle of the morning!

And I kept asking him the same question, *"Where did you find that animal?"* Evidently, Todd had been rummaging along the back fence that ran beside the creek bed. He saw the tiny dead animal and somehow managed to drag it through the fence so that he could give it to me as a gift instead of breaking off another flower from my garden.

What a child! What a great thinker! What a terrific kid to care so much for his mother that he went to all the trouble to scavenge the creek bed for a dead rat!

After the cleansing, fresh clothes, and a snack, I settled my son down for a nap and tried to figure out what to do about that dead thing lying in front of my house.

Stepping outside, I looked around the yard and saw a big stick lying under the tree. Using that stick, I pushed the critter until it dropped off my walkway into the street gutter. Going back into the house, I called the city's animal control department and asked them to come and get the dead rat.

They arrived promptly, investigated the creek bed behind the fence in the backyard, and assured me that the dead critter was **not** a rat and that I did not need to worry about there being rats in the creek. They *said* it was not a rat, but they could not tell me for sure what kind of animal this used to be. Maybe it was a baby raccoon, maybe a possum. It had been dead so long they did not know what it was! However, they did tell me that there was no evidence of any more of them anywhere near my house. I was not sure whether to be relieved or on guard.

Later, I told my son how much I appreciated his little gifts of love every day and asked if he wanted to plant his own special garden of flowers. When they grew, he could pick as many of them as he wanted every day. That is exactly what we did.

Oh, the love of a mother for her child! It transcends common sense! It is watchful, willing to scrub away the dirt, and never afraid to poke a rat with a stick. A mother's love is bigger than dead critters and broken flower stems. He is my child, and I love him unconditionally.

Such is the love of God for His children. How wonderful to know that God loves us completely, even when we proudly present Him with a dead critter instead of a fragrant bouquet.

Romans 8:39
"Nor height, nor depth, nor any other creature, shall be able to separate us from the love of God, which is in Christ Jesus our Lord." (KJV)

LF

What's a Mother To Do?

Ialways took my children with me, regardless of where I was going. It could be to the grocery store, drug store, shopping center, doctor's office, restaurant, and of course, church. Usually, they were well behaved, and I had no trouble getting in, taking care of my business, and getting back out.

One day, I was hurrying through the grocery store aisles with Marci, two years old, perched up in the seat of the shopping cart, and Todd, five years old, walking along beside me. I knew exactly what I needed and stayed on-course throughout the store. With two children in the grocery store, I could easily get sidetracked and end up with a bunch of stuff in the cart that I had not planned to buy.

As we turned the corner into the frozen foods section, we ran into Mrs. Bodsford, a nice lady who lived near us. Stopping briefly, we said good morning, and how are you, and nice to see you. She commented how pretty Marci was, and what a handsome boy Todd was, and then we said goodbye and moved on our way.

As I continued down the frozen food aisle, Todd saw the ice cream displays. *"Mommy, buy us some ice cream,"* he asked.

"No, Todd, not today. It's not on my list, and we have ice cream in the freezer at home," I said.

Evidently, Mrs. Bodsford heard my son ask for the ice cream, but she did not hear all of my reply. She only heard me say, *"No, Todd, not today. It's not on my list…"* She must have assumed that I did not have enough money to pay for ice cream, and that was the reason I did not buy any for the children.

Being the nice lady that she was, she turned her cart around and came up beside me. Grabbing my hand, she tucked several dollars into my palm and said, *"Now you buy those babies some ice cream. They need a little treat every now and then."* Before I could say a word, she hurried off.

I was so embarrassed and also a little annoyed. I had already told my child *"No,"* and he was satisfied with my answer. Should I go back on my word and put the ice cream in the cart? Had Todd heard what Mrs. Bodsford said, and did he know she gave me money for ice cream? I did not want my children to get the idea that someone could intervene and override their parents' decisions. Even something as insignificant as whether to buy ice cream could make an impression on my young children.

I made up my mind and said nothing further about it. Finishing the shopping, I put the groceries and the children in the car and drove home.

Later that day, I handed Todd the dollars that Mrs. Bodsford had given me in the grocery store and said, *"Mrs. Bodsford gave you money for ice cream. Put this money in your piggy bank, and the next time the ice cream truck comes down the street, you can use this money to buy some."*

It is not easy to tell our children *"No,"* especially with the world around them yelling *"YES!"* Likewise, the next time God says *"No"* to you, accept it without complaint. Just like a parent, He knows what is best for His child.

Proverbs 3:5-6
"Trust in the Lord with all thine heart; and lean not unto thine own understanding. In all thy ways acknowledge him, and he shall direct thy paths." (KJV)

LF

"Nana, Do You Love Me?"

"*N*ana," said my grandson Zachary. *"Do you love me when I'm not here?"*

I looked into his eyes and saw the question lingering in his gaze. This child was serious, and no doubt, the question had been on his mind for a while.

Children are so direct and so honest. They will tell you exactly what they are thinking and hold nothing back.

Picking him up, I held him on my lap and hugged him close to my heart. With his head nestled on my shoulder, I said, *"Zachary, I love you when you are here with me, and I love you when you are not here. I love you always, no matter where you are. My love for you is kind of like God's love for all His children. Even though He is not physically with us, we know He loves us completely and that He is always with us in Spirit."*

"Nana, I love you all the time too!" said Zachary. With a smile and a hug, he jumped off my lap and ran off to play. Then, he stopped and called to me one last time, *"Nana, I'll be back soon. But you're not alone. You can talk to God until I get back."*

And I did.

Jeremiah 31:3
"...I have loved you with an everlasting love..." (NIV)

LF

Go Ahead and Cuddle

My husband purchased a piece of jewelry for me at a local jewelry store as a Christmas gift. The next day, I took the ring back to the store to have it resized.

The sales lady that waited on me was the same person that assisted Dave when he bought the ring. As she measured my finger and arranged to have the ring cut down to my size, she said, *"I remember your husband. You are a lucky lady. In fact, we were all talking about you after your husband left the store."*

Naturally, I was curious and asked her to tell me what had been said about Dave and me.

She said, *"We have a teenage girl working part-time, and she was here when your husband bought the ring. After he left the store, she told us that she goes to the same church as you do and that you and your husband sit up near the front of the auditorium every Sunday all cuddled up together. She told us that every time she sees you and your husband, you are holding hands, or he has his arm around you."*

Talk about setting an example! Cuddling with my husband fulfilled Titus 2:4-5.

Titus 2:4-5
"Then they can train the younger women to love their husbands and children, to be self-controlled and pure, to be busy at home, to be kind, and to be subject to their husbands, so that no one will malign the word of God." (NIV)

This was a good reminder that people are watching! You never know who might observe what you do or see something in your life that will make an impression.

LF

Attitude Giggles

Clean Up in the Produce Department

Grocery shopping is not at the top of my "fun things to do" list. If I never had to do it again, it would be all right with me. I get in, get done, get out! Just think of the time people would save if they didn't have to eat. And don't get me started on the money we would save. That, however, is another story so let's not go any farther than we already have.

I was in the grocery store and was caught off guard by these beautiful blueberries. I don't like blueberries that much, but they just got hold of me and wouldn't let go. Before I knew what had happened, I was standing, yes standing, in an ocean of blueberries. No, I wasn't dreaming. I was wide awake during this nightmare. The blueberries were in little see-through containers, all stacked neatly and at a very interesting slant. I picked up one package, and then it started. They were all headed south, and I couldn't stop them. I could only hang on to the one container in my hand and watch as dozens of other containers hit the floor and burst open! I had no idea that blueberries could roll that fast and far.

A lady watched as all this took place around me. I turned and looked at her and she said, *"I'm going for help."*

"Thank you," I replied. I couldn't move a foot. There was no place to step without scrunching blueberries under my feet. Somebody had to come and pick them up and fast. Just as I turned, I saw Frank from my church standing at the door of the store, heading out. Oh yes, this was at the front of the store where everybody entering and leaving the store could get in on the action of the run-a-way blueberries!

Looking at him, I said, *"Frank, you get out of here and not a word of this to a single person or else!"* Of all the people in the United States of America and all foreign countries that I didn't want to see me stuck there in the middle of an ocean of run-a-way blueberries, it was Frank! He has a way of ribbing you even if he doesn't have a single thing to rib you about. He left, smiling like a Cheshire cat. Help came and freed me from the blueberries. I went home more convinced than ever about how much I didn't like grocery shopping.

The next morning in church, I had this notice in my choir folder slot:

CLEAN UP
IN THE PRODUCE AISLE
DUE TO
CLUTSY CUSTOMER!

I didn't have to think twice to know who had authored this piece of work: FRANK! The news had spread through the church like those blueberries had spread over the floor of the produce department.

I'm glad that I am part of a church family where we can laugh at and with one another. Did Frank make me mad? No! Not at all! I fully expected him to tell that tale to the first person he saw, and he didn't disappoint me. Family is a wonderful thing to be a part of, but your spiritual family is a special part of life.

If you don't know the joy of a wonderful church family, don't let another day pass by that you do not decide in your heart that you need one. Oh, the blessing and fun you can have. You never know when you too will end up in an ocean of run-a-way blueberries, and you just might need someone to laugh with.

As the song by William Gaither says, *"I'm so glad I'm a part of the Family of God."*

Ephesians 4:25
"Therefore each of you must put off falsehood and speak truthfully to his neighbor, for we are all members of one body." (NIV)

PS

Don't Clean It Up

"I have got to have some help! This house needs to be cleaned top to bottom, the laundry is piling up, we are eating fast food every night, and the floors need a good session with the vacuum cleaner!"

I was having my own little whining session and was on a roll. The problem was that no one was listening to me. Nobody was home! As I stood in the midst of this messy house and viewed the unwashed dishes on the counter and the crumbs on the floor, I knew that my teenagers had been home for lunch and did not take the time to clean up after themselves.

I cannot stand a dirty house! Desperation set in as I walked from room to room, taking assessment of the housework that needed to be done. My heart sank as I realized I just did not have time to clean the house.

My husband was on a business trip, working in Germany on a ten-week assignment, and I had a plane to catch in two hours that would take me to New York for a Human Resources Conference. I thought about missing the conference and staying home but knew that was not the best idea.

I was pulled in every direction. My house was a disaster, my husband was away on business, I had a full-time job, and I was also working toward my Ph.D. I had research to do, a thesis to write, and a presentation to make. Plus, I had those three teenagers to keep track of. They all had part-time jobs after school and homework to finish, and I wanted them to concentrate on making good grades.

I sank to the floor and gazed around the room. How was I going to manage all these things and make sure nothing was left undone?

Then I had an inspiration. I picked up the phone book and searched for the number of an acquaintance who owned a house cleaning service.

I called her and asked if she could possibly work me into her busy schedule. *"I only need someone to clean the bathrooms and the kitchen; I can take care of the rest,"* I said with assurance.

She agreed to re-arrange her schedule and said she would have someone there on Tuesday the next week.

What a relief! Finally, I would get some help. I quickly threw some clothes in a bag and drove to the airport. Why hadn't I done this sooner?

Many times my husband Dave had offered to hire someone to help in the house, but I had always refused, telling him that I could take care of it myself. Dave is a tremendous help, but he would be gone for many weeks. Hiring a cleaning person would surely take the pressure off me, and I decided that I would offer her the job every week.

The following Monday night, I went to bed thinking about the cleaning person that would come to the house the next morning. Maybe I should just check those bathrooms and make sure there were not towels on the floor or toothpaste stuck in the sink.

So I got up out of bed, went to each bathroom, and began to straighten up. I decided to go ahead and wipe the counters, collect the laundry, and empty the trash containers. Moving through each bathroom, I wiped down the mirrors, cleaned the toilets and showers, and rinsed down the bathtubs.

A couple of hours later, I made my way to the kitchen. Just as I expected, it needed help! I unloaded and reloaded the dishwasher, swept the floor, and ran the mop over the linoleum.

Satisfied with my efforts, I washed up and went back to bed. It was 3 o'clock in the morning.

When the alarm went off two hours later, I was still laying there trying to go to sleep. I realized I had worked myself into a frenzy and had been too wound up to go to sleep. I crawled out of bed and was glad that there was nothing to do to get ready for the cleaning person. She would be there at 8 a.m., and I headed off for the office, proud that she would see what a clean house I really had.

Do you see the irony in this? As I yawned through the day, it suddenly dawned on me what I had done. I cleaned up so the cleaning person would not see the mess. The reason I hired her was to clean the house, yet I did not allow her to do it. Did I think I was fooling her and that she would not figure out what I had done? Sadly, I was just too proud to admit that I was not Super Woman.

I wonder if we try to fool God and other people in the same way. Is there dirt in our lives that we sweep into the corner and then try to clean it ourselves?

Most people have done it at some time in their lives. They dress up pretty, put on cologne, paste a smile on their faces, and drive to church. They stroll around greeting people, pray in *"Jesus' Name,"* teach a Sunday School Class, listen carefully during the preaching, and sing loud and sweet. Then, they get in the car to leave. On the way home, they fuss at the kids, criticize their spouse, and complain about anything that comes to mind. They are covering up the dirt!

Don't clean it up yourself! That is only a temporary fix. Allow God to cleanse your heart. Our only source of true cleansing comes from Him.

And let the cleaning people do their job. They will thank you for it every time you write the check.

Psalm 51:10
"Create in me a clean heart, O God; and renew a right spirit within me." (KJV)

LF

The Mystery Trip

I love spending time with my mother, and we have made it a priority over the years to take a day or two and go somewhere together. One of our favorite things to do is to go on Mystery Trips.

A Mystery Trip is when you get on a big bus with about 50 other women and not know where you are headed. You do not find out where you are going until you actually get there.

One year, our Mystery Trip took us to the Inner Harbor in Baltimore; another year, we spent three days in Charleston, SC. Still another time, we ended up on top of a mountain in West Virginia and rode a train backwards down the mountain.

However, there is one Mystery Trip that stands out in my mind as the most memorable trip. We got up at 3:30 on a Saturday morning so that we could be on the bus at 5 a.m. The bus left promptly, and all the women on the bus were passing around homemade goodies, laughing and talking, and guessing where we would go for the day.

The bus was heading south, and I was certain we were going to Myrtle Beach. I couldn't wait! I love the beach, I love the shows, and I love the shopping. Convinced of our destination, I closed my eyes and tried to take a little nap so that I would be refreshed for the day ahead.

Sure enough, the bus crossed over into South Carolina but did not take the highway toward the beach. The bus continued south and then turned toward the mountains. Mom and I knew we had gone into unfamiliar territory. I was on alert from there on.

That bus kept going and kept going, and I did not think we were ever going to get there. We drove for over six hours! People were getting antsy, but the tour director kept assuring us that we were on the right road and that we would have a wonderful day and a great time at our final destination.

Just before noon, the big bus pulled off onto a dirt side road and headed down the long drive up to a large farmhouse. Mom and I thought the driver must be lost and was stopping to ask for directions. No such thing; we had arrived!

As the women unloaded off the bus, we received our itineraries for the day. The plan was to tour a Goat Farm! My mother started laughing as she watched me standing there with this incredulous, dumbfounded look on my face. I could not believe this was happening!

A Goat Farm! Why in the world would I want to ride six hours on a bus so that I could look at goats? I don't know anything about goats, never wanted to know anything about goats. I thought we were going shopping.

They walked us from corral to corral, pointing out the various mama goats, baby goats, and daddy goats. To top off our goat farm experience, we were offered the unique opportunity to buy goat soap, goat lotion, and goat milk.

As my mother and the other ladies "Ooh'ed" and "Ahh'ed" over the goats and goat products, I stood off by myself under a tree, fuming. I had spent all that money for this trip so that Mom and I could have a lovely day together, and we ended up on a goat farm!

I was so disappointed and frustrated. The thought of spending six hours riding back home was annoying. I just stood there under the tree and tried to stay in the shade. It was a scorching hot day, and I did not want to be tramping around in the goat corral in that heat, not to mention the smell.

When we got back on the bus, we were handed a boxed lunch, and everyone settled in for the journey home. I told Mom I was sorry the trip turned out so bad.

She just smiled at me and said, *"You know, honey, it doesn't matter to me where we go. I just want to spend time with you."*

She was right! My mother is so sweet and such a blessing to me. Yet, I had wasted half the day already by pouting and complaining rather than taking advantage of having my mother all to myself.

For the rest of the journey, we laughed and talked and had a marvelous time. We joined in the merriment with the other women on the bus. Just imagine, 50 women on a bus! That is a rocking good time.

This story reminds me of Jonah. He certainly went on a trip but not on a bus. Jonah went in the belly of a whale. He was spit up by the whale, seated under a gourd tree, and left standing in the heat of the day. He was so mad! When Jonah cooled off and settled down, he saw that his problem was not his physical location, it was his mental attitude. When he got a grip on that, he had fun.

I look forward to my next Mystery Trip with my mother, and I do not care where we go. I want to spend every available moment with my mother while she is still with me. Bring it on!

Philippians 4:11
"...for I have learned to be content whatever the circumstances." (NIV)

LF

The Joy of Pulling Weeds

Zachary had earned $5.00 by hitting a grand slam homerun in the Little League ballgame. Naturally, I was the person who paid the child for this remarkable performance! But that is what grandmothers do.

The $5.00 was safely tucked in his wallet, and he could not wait to spend it. The next Sunday after we gathered for family lunch at my house, Zachary pulled me aside and said, *"Hey, Nana, will you take me to a store so I can buy something with my money?"* Jackson was standing there as well so I loaded both boys in my car and off we drove to the nearest store I could find – Walgreens.

Walking through the aisles of Walgreens, we found the small supply of toys. Zachary was quick to decide on a tub of putty for only $2.00. Jackson was not so quick. He picked up and investigated every toy, every book, everything he could get his hands on. No amount of prodding helped hurry this child along.

Finally, I said to Jackson, *"Pick out something right now. We have to go. Your daddy is waiting on us."*

I offered to buy Jackson two little cars, and he agreed. We went to the front of the store toward the cash register with Zachary leading the way.

Proudly, Zachary stepped up and paid for his tub of putty with his own money. Then I paid for Jackson's cars. Just as the clerk was putting the toys in a bag, Jackson changed his mind!

Jackson said *"NO! I don't want that. I want a different toy!"*

I said, *"Jackson, we already decided on these two cars and do not have time to go back and look again."*

That sweet baby looked me straight in my face and immediately threw himself on the floor of the Walgreens. He started screaming and crying and banging and kicking and demanding and having himself a good, old-fashioned kind of fit right in the middle of the store!

People stopped what they were doing. All cash register transactions ceased, and a small crowd gathered at the end of each aisle to watch this three year old lying on the floor. Some people glared at me, as if I had done something to hurt the child. Others were snickering; still others were handing out criticisms, such as *"My child would NEVER act that way."*

Zachary was mortified! He backed toward the door and said, *"Come on. Let's get out of here."* I wanted to get out of there too! But getting Jackson out of there was a different story. He refused to move, stand up, stop crying, or allow me to pick him up.

I could not physically lift him off the floor. The more I tried to coerce him into stopping the tantrum, the louder he got. I handed my purse to Zachary, reached down, and grabbed Jackson under each shoulder. Then, I literally dragged him across the floor and out the door.

Once outside, standing in the pouring rain, I had to drag that child across the parking lot to the car. It was a struggle of wills! Nevertheless, I managed to get both boys safely strapped into the car, and we were on the way home.

Jackson cried most of the way, and I did not even try to reason with him. When he finally realized that he was not going to get his own way by throwing a fit, the crying and kicking stopped, and his tantrum was over.

He took the two little cars and played with them all afternoon and had a wonderful time! I watched this child in amazement. He had never displayed this kind of behavior before. He had always been calm, rational, sweet, loving, and even-tempered.

Suddenly, this *"weed"* of discontentment sprouted up in him, and I was forced to deal with it.

Don't we all deal with weeds in our gardens? We take all the right steps to ensure the weeds do not grow in the first place; but when they do, we want them gone! We immediately pull them out so they do not spoil the garden.

God is the same way. He sees us with loving, fatherly eyes; yet He is quick to pull those weeds when we act-out or throw an adult tantrum. God loves us so much.

There is more than one way to get rid of the weeds. Sometimes you might have to DRAG them out! Get them out anyway you can. They have no place in the garden.

Oh, the joy of pulling weeds.

2 Timothy 3:16
"All scripture is given by inspiration of God, and is profitable for doctrine, for reproof, for correction, for instruction in righteousness." (KJV)

LF

Stepping on the Stones

Has it ever happened to you? You feel inspired to create something, write something, volunteer for a project, or try to do something new, and suddenly you are hit with criticism from somebody who is doing nothing? It is as if that person is sitting there, waiting for you to make a move so that they can say something negative about it.

The day I wrote my first few lines of poetry, someone said to me, *"You're just on an ego trip."* So mortified that anyone would think of me that way, I put away my pen and paper and did not try to write anything again for several years.

In fact, 20 years ago when my first poems were published in *Paths Less Traveled* through the Library of Congress, I did not tell anyone! Even today, no one in my family has a copy of the book; I have never presented the book at any book fair or book signing or tried to market the book in anyway.

It is not that I am ashamed of the work. Writing those poems helped me express myself during some of the darkest days of my life. But at that time, I allowed one person's sarcastic comment to throw a stone through my self-confidence. Instead of stepping on the stone and moving on, I allowed the stone to hurt my feelings.

Why do some people take pleasure in hurting others? Some people are so insecure within themselves, they actually feel better by putting other people down. They gain a feeling of superiority by blaming, criticizing, and complaining.

There are people who go through their life stating, *"I would NEVER do that,"* and aiming their cruel words at people who are dealing with sensitive issues and doing their best to cope and maintain. A prime example of this is people who throw darts at parents trying to raise children and say, *"I would never let my children do that."*

Some people get pleasure from their own negativity. They never look around for service opportunities but are quick to judge and make snide remarks about people who are stepping out there and trying. There is nothing supportive or sincere about their motives. They are like a pebble in your shoe.

I want to be a person that others use as a "stepping stone to success" rather than become a pebble in their shoes, causing pain in their lives. I want to be the one that God uses to lighten the load and bear the burden for someone who is struggling.

God, help us to be stepping stones in the garden of our lives.

Hebrews 6:10
"God is not unjust; he will not forget your work and the love you have shown him as you have helped his people and continue to help them." (NIV)

LF

Laugh Anyway!

T he woman in my office was upset. She was having a bad day and going through a relationship problem. She appeared to be stressed and self-absorbed. She sat there telling me all about it and blaming everyone else but herself.

During any counseling session, my goal is to listen and give practical advice. So I began providing her with stress management techniques that could help her cope with her situation.

Upon hearing this, she became quite angry with me and shouted, *"You obviously do not understand what I am going through! How could you possibly know how I feel?"* She went on to accuse me of giving her flimsy and useless advice and doing nothing to help her.

Surprised at her outburst and even more surprised that she was blaming me, I realized how ironic the whole conversation was. She did not know me at all and thought that no one else in the world had ever experienced problems or bad times.

I could not help it. I just started laughing. I tried to suppress the giggles, but I could not.

Have you ever been around someone who was rolling with laughter? Before you know it, you start laughing too? That is exactly what happened. First, she started gently coughing with her hand up over her mouth, trying to contain her own laughter. She did not want me to know that my laughter was contagious, and she caught it!

After a few moments, she began to giggle. She kept saying, *"What's so funny?"* And soon she was laughing aloud; we were laughing together.

I was finally able to regain control of myself and knew I would need to take a more direct approach with this gal and give her a good dose of reality.

I said, *"Believe me, Sister, I DO understand. Tell me, have you ever lost it all? Ever been beat-up, knocked down, and held down? Ever had a broken heart, lost someone you loved, your job, and your mind? Ever been so down and out you could not afford to feed your kids?"*

She stopped giggling and sat there with her mouth open and eyes wide in amazement. *"You have never experienced those things either,"* she threw at me.

"Yes, all those, plus many more! Don't tell me I don't understand and can't put myself in your place. I've been there...and back," I said sternly, no longer laughing or smiling.

She sat quietly, thoughtfully, for a moment, and then a sheepish grin crept to her face. I could tell the reality had set in, and she finally "got it." Now she was ready and willing to hear what I had to say that might possibly help her deal with her stress.

As we continued through the session, I focused on helping her put things in perspective. She realized that her problems were not as overpowering as she thought they were and that other people have problems too. She was not alone.

God will not put more on us than we are able to bear, and He will always provide a way to escape. It is important to keep your sense of humor! Being able to laugh in times of trouble will keep you grounded and sane.

Job 8:21
"He will yet fill your mouth with laughter and your lips with shouts of joy." (NIV)

LF

"I Didn't Know the Rule"

Will was my very first piano student. I started teaching during my senior year of college. My piano was in my living room, and that is where I would teach. I was very nervous when the time came for Will to arrive for his first lesson. I even changed clothes three times. What was a piano teacher supposed to look like anyway? I hadn't had a piano teacher for a long time and had forgotten how they were supposed to look.

Will was a cute little boy of the ripe ol' age of six years. This little guy was a perfectionist. He wanted to do everything right the first time. He could read music with the best of the six year olds.

During one of his lessons, he kept making the same mistake over and over. Although trying, he just couldn't get it. Without warning, this mild-mannered little boy had a fit. He banged my piano, sassed me when I told him not to do that, jumped off the bench, ran under my dining room table, and from there he ran into the foyer and under another table. All of this happened so fast I couldn't stop him!

And I was afraid that Will would find his way under the massive green sheet in the corner covering my Christmas tree that I hadn't had time to take down yet (this was May). If he had turned that tree over, we would still be climbing out from under the pile of fake tree limbs and broken ornaments! Finally, he ended up crouched under that table like a bird caught in a trap. This little blonde-haired "bird" had just fluttered his way into complete exhaustion.

I pounced like a cat on that little bird! I was mad as a firecracker! I snarled, *"Will, you get back here right this minute! Sit yourself back on this piano bench, and you listen to me, young man. Don't you ever bang my piano again! Don't you ever sass me again, and don't you ever leave this piano bench again until your lesson is over! Do you understand me?"*

I don't know who was more shocked at what I had just said, me or Will. I had always been so calm and sweet. I didn't know that I had it in me, but I guess I did.

Will looked up at me, almost in tears (he was not the only one), and said to me, *"You don't like me anymore."*

I assured him that I did like him. I just needed to make sure that this sort of thing never happened again. Then Will said something that changed my whole outlook on everyday life.

He said, *"I didn't know the rule; if I had known the rule, I would not have broken it."*

Well, howdy! Now whenever I meet new students for the first time, I tell them the rules. From that day to this, I have tried to make sure that everyone in my life knows the rules (family, students, and all those who I interact with).

I want to be sure that I know the rules that my family and friends have for me. Most of all, I want to know the rules that my Heavenly Father has for me.

Do the people in your life a favor! Tell them the rules. Do yourself a favor and know God's rules. Wouldn't it be a wonderful place if we all knew the rules and followed them? Will, I will be forever grateful for the lesson you taught me that day.

Psalm 66:7
"He rules forever by his power, his eyes watch the nations—let not the rebellious rise up against him." (NIV)

2 Timothy 2:5
"Similarly, if anyone competes as an athlete, he does not receive the victor's crown unless he competes according to the rules." (NIV)

PS

Character Giggles

What a Pair

I walked into the church, got my choir book, and went to the choir room. This is what you do and where you go when you sing in the adult choir of our church.

I had just sat down when my good friend Felicia said, *"Phyllis, you have something on the back of your skirt."*

My skirt was a dark, royal blue color. How could anything show on that? I went into the ladies' room and pulled my skirt around to see for myself what was there. Sure enough, there was a white smudge of something unrecognizable.

By that time, Sharon and Felicia were with me, and I said, *"Let's get a towel and try to wash it off."*

Sharon said, *"No, just leave it. Washing it will leave a bigger mess."*

Agreeing with her suggestion, I left it alone, and we went back into the choir room. I had decided that this had come from one of the children who sings in my children's choir. It was just at the level where a child would hug me around my legs. I was sure they had some type of candy on their hands. If this was the worse thing that could happen as a result of being a children's choir director, then I would wear the candy on my skirt with pride.

We left the choir room and headed for the sanctuary. Another lady said, *"Phyllis, you have something on your skirt."*

I said, *"I think it is candy from a child's hug."*

Before I could reach the sanctuary, two more ladies told me about my *dirty, horrible, candy-stained* skirt. Wasn't anybody being noticed today but me?

I finally made it to the choir loft. When we were shaking hands and greeting everyone, like Baptists are so famous for, three more people gave me a skirt report. By this time, I was getting a little bit concerned about whether I should even have come to church that morning. I was, however, certain that I shouldn't have worn that skirt.

When I left the choir loft and went to my seat on the pew beside my husband, you guessed it, a voice from behind, *"Phyllis, you have something on your skirt."*

As we were walking to Sunday School, I told my husband, *"Let's run and hurry and sit down."*

We did, but not before I heard, *"Phyllis, you have something on your skirt."*

After Sunday School, I told my husband, *"I want to sneak out during the closing prayer. If one more person tells me about my nasty skirt, I am going to scream."*

The folks at church that morning were surely following Paul's instructions to Timothy when he said, *"Those who sin are to be rebuked publicly, so that others may take warning,"* (1Timothy 5:20 NIV).

I wish they had remembered God's instructions to Samuel instead: *"...'Do not consider his appearance...The Lord does not look at the things man looks at. Man looks at the outward appearance, but the Lord looks at the heart,'"* (1 Samuel 16:7 NIV).

That was all the church I could handle for one day! Home at last! I went immediately to my room to get out of that skirt. Well, just when I thought things could not get worse, they did! I had just taken off the skirt when I heard my husband laughing and calling for me to come quick.

I thought, *"What has happened now!"* I was not in the mood to laugh about anything. I hoped that whatever it was, I would be able to fake a laugh. But I didn't have to fake anything.

He said, *"Will you just look at my shoes?"* I did. He was wearing two different shoes!

He had been at church as long as I had that morning, and no one had said a word to him about his mismatched shoes! At least my shoes matched! But even if they hadn't, no one would have noticed because my skirt was just too hideous! The two of us were quite a pair that Sunday morning. Too bad his shoes weren't!

At the end of the day, I guess Paul was right: *"The sins of some men are obvious...the sins of others trail behind them,"* (1 Timothy 5:24 NIV). I wonder if Paul realized that some sins could be both obvious and trail behind us! What a pair!

Matthew 7:1-5

"'Do not judge, or you too will be judged. For in the same way you judge others, you will be judged, and with the measure you use, it will be measured to you. Why do you look at the speck of sawdust in your brother's eye and pay no attention to the plank in your own eye? How can you say to your brother, "Let me take the speck out of your eye," when all the time there is a plank in your own eye? You hypocrite, first take the plank out of your own eye, and then you will see clearly to remove the speck from your brother's eye.'" (NIV)

PS

What's Your Name?

hildren's minds are like little sponges as they are growing up, just waiting to draw in everything that comes their way. They will learn whatever we make an effort to teach them. When my son Brian was a baby, I began teaching him a Bible verse. I chose Philippians 4:19 (KJV): *"But my God shall supply all your need according to his riches in glory by Christ Jesus."*

I chose this verse because it speaks volumes in just a few words. If Brian never learned another verse of scripture in his life, I knew that this verse said it all. Brian needed to know that God was his sufficiency in everything and that Christ Jesus was the only way to inherit the riches of God.

I would repeat this verse to him when I was bathing him, feeding him, changing him, and just playing with him. After he began talking, I would say, *"Brian what is your verse?"*

Brian would quietly say, *"Philippians 4:19."* Later he began to say, *"Philippians 4:19,"* and then quote the entire verse. I can't tell you the times I would ask him, *"Brian, what's your verse?"*

One day I took him to the mall to have his picture made. The lady placed him on the table and was getting his little shirt and pants straightened just right. She was so gentle and kind that it was easy to tell that she really liked children. She was also good at what she was doing.

And then she began the question, *"What's your...,"* but she didn't get to finish her question, which would have been *"What's your name?"* because Brian immediately answered *"Philippians 4:19."* I bet she had never heard that before!

I quickly answered, *"His name is Brian."* I acted like I hadn't heard a word he had said. She made his picture, and I took him home. He was well trained, or should I say, programmed.

As I was reading in my Bible one day, I noticed that I had circled Philippians 4:19 and put a note by it that said *"Brian's verse."* I looked, and there on the same page in my Bible, I had circled Philippians 4:13 (KJV), *"I can do all things through Christ which strengtheneth me,"* and had put a note by it: *"Jodie's verse."*

Brian and Jodie were married four years ago in 2003. Isn't it just like God to put two people together who already had their life's verses on the same page? It was always thrilling to hear this little guy quoting his Bible verse before he could hardly talk. But what is really exciting is to watch him and his wife as they live out both their life's verses while they serve the Lord together.

Psalm 119:11
"Thy word have I hid in mine heart, that I might not sin against thee." (KJV)

PS

Cell Phones Can't Swim

When cell phones first came around, I thought they were the most unnecessary instruments that had ever been made by man. I would look over at other drivers as they were talking on the phone in their cars and think, *"How crazy is that? Who in the world needs a telephone in their car? I'm glad to get in my car and know that no one can get to me. This is my time. I will never have a phone in my car."*

Those words still ring in my head every time my cell phone rings in my purse! I even went so far as to tell my friends, *"If you ever see me with a phone at my ear in my car, drag me off to the funny farm because I will be ready to go!"*

Well, like every other person on the planet, I have a cell phone. Thank goodness my friends didn't remember what I said about the funny farm. I'm still here.

Recently, my husband and I were in Florida on vacation. I love to walk on the beach. He was going for a run, and I was going for a walk. I wanted to take my cell phone just in case he needed me before I got back. I wore my bathing suit so that after walking I could jump right into the pool. I didn't have any pockets in my cover up so I put my phone in the "top part" of my bathing suit.

I had a great walk, but hot wasn't the word for it! So it was to the pool as quickly as I could possibly get there, showering of course before entering. Even that felt wonderful! But did you notice: Cell phone shower number one!

Then into the pool we went: my cell phone and me! And you guessed it. I had forgotten all about having that thing!

I was in the pool for a long and relaxing time. The cell phone didn't ring; the first shower probably did it in, but I'm not sure that the ring could have been heard under water anyway. I don't swim, but I sure do like floating around on this long tubular contraption called a "noodle," which, by the way, is a great invention for a non-swimmer like me.

I finally left the pool and headed for the room. I like to get into the shower with my bathing suit on and rinse the chlorine out before taking it off. And you guessed it: Cell phone shower number two!

Well, what do you know, when the bathing suit came off, the cell phone hit the shower floor! Only then did I remember that I had put that thing there. Oh well, just mark it up to another uncontrollable, goofed up again, why can't I remember, "senior moment!"

I felt like flushing that thing down the toilet and asking everybody, *"Have you seen my cell phone?"* A "side-ways lie" would be better than the truth about this one! But I didn't do that. I just picked it up, handed it to my husband, and confessed.

If he had asked me, *"Phyllis, why did you take your cell phone into the pool?"* I think I would have had a major "hissy fit," but thank goodness he didn't. He was very kind about it. He even said he might have done the same thing. Just think about it. How in the world would he have done the same thing? I put it in the top of my bathing suit! Oh well, I did appreciate his kindness. The phone was destroyed, even though he worked hours trying to dry it out with the hair dryer.

I had not been without a cell phone in years until this trip to Florida. We were gone for two weeks, and this happened during the first week. I called my brothers on my husband's phone and told them that I had taken my phone swimming, and now it wouldn't work. If they needed me, they could call me on Guy's phone.

Our first Sunday back at church after our trip, a friend came up to me in the parking lot. As we were walking into the church she said, *"Phyllis, I heard you took your cell phone swimming!"*

Now just tell me how that story of my stupidity got home before I did? I think there is a lesson here. Remember, no matter how far away from home you travel, behave yourself. News, good or bad, can travel faster than you can. Even without your cell phone!

And I think there's another lesson here. I cannot tell you how much I missed that stupid contraption! I have had to eat my first words about a cell phone time and time again. Remember to keep your words "sweet" because more than likely you will be eating most of them.

Numbers 32:23
"...and you may be sure that your sin will find you out." (NIV)

Proverbs 16:24
"Pleasant words are a honeycomb, sweet to the soul and healing to the bones." (NIV)

PS

Are You Like a Turtle?

Would you like to be compared to a turtle? Probably not and it may be because there are not many known quotes about this animal.

We have all heard the more notable, popular quotes about other animals, and we use the examples every day. We make comparisons based on the characteristics of the animals, such as:

- Gentle as a lamb
- Sly as a fox
- Soar like an eagle
- Sting like a bee
- Wise as an owl
- Busy as a beaver
- Proud as a peacock
- Roar like a lion
- Clever as a crow
- Fast as a shark
- Swift as a rabbit
- Slow as a snail
- Strong as an ox
- Stubborn as a mule
- Float like a butterfly
- Work like a dog
- Mean as a snake
- Scaredy-cat
- Bird-brained
- And so on…

But what do we know about turtles? Is there anything to be learned from their characteristics?

First, a turtle has a shell. They can go completely into their shell and shut it up tightly. Each turtle's shell has a different pattern or design so it is customized to that turtle.

The turtle uses his shell for protection. It is a place to hide, shelter from the weather, or even a storage place. The primary reason for the shell, however, is to protect the turtle from predators.

Turtles enjoy a carefree life as long as they stay inside their shells. They exist in calm surroundings with little interaction with the world around them.

One lesson we can learn from the turtle is that <u>he only makes progress when he sticks his neck out.</u> He must come out of his shell to move forward!

Are you hiding inside your shell? Stuck in your own protected surroundings away from the world and unwilling to take any risks in your life?

If so, you are not fulfilling your purpose in life. You may be afraid of taking a risk, exposing yourself to possible failure, or even afraid of winning. Interestingly, some people are more afraid of being successful than they are of making a mistake.

If something scares you, that is even more reason to do it! You will never make progress in your life if you do not step out on faith and take a chance. God will not call you to do the work without providing the means for you to do it.

He did not intend for us to live inside our shells, or our comfort zone. We become complacent, sitting back, waiting for others to step forward and do the work. God said in John 4:35 (NIV), *"...open your eyes and look at the fields! They are ripe for harvest."* There is much work to do, yet we sit comfortably inside our shells and do nothing.

You will never know the joy of a life of purpose unless there is purpose in your life.

2 Timothy 1:7 and 9
"For God hath not given us the spirit of fear; but of power, and of love, and of a sound mind...Who hath saved us, and called us with an holy

calling...according to his own purpose and grace, which was given us in Christ Jesus..." (KJV)

LF

Are You Missing the Bus?

Your life is cruising along at high speed, and you think you have everything under control. Although your daily schedule is hectic, you have a system in place to maintain some degree of organization, and everyone in your family seems to be cooperating nicely.

This is a breeze! Just put some structure to it, and you can do it all. Or so it seems. You just plod along, taking care of the house, taking care of your job, taking care of the kids, taking care of the husband, taking care of the church functions, taking care…taking care…taking care… taking care.

You believe you have it all covered. Then suddenly, without any warning whatsoever, some small little kink will appear in your perfectly structured life. Your normally organized schedule disappears, and chaos reigns. You wonder what happened, and you begin to get agitated.

Somebody must have done *something* to mess up my routine *on purpose!* I must find the guilty party and let them have it! How dare they burden me with figuring out how to "fix it." The problem could be something simple: child misses the school bus, or you realize the gas tank is almost empty on your way to work.

Your first step is to find out *who* is to blame for the problem. Let's see…you would not be in danger of running out of gas in the car if your husband had filled it up the night before. Off you dash to the phone to inform him of his mistake, and the day is off to a great start! He listens with astonishment as you hurl accusations at him and help him understand the hardship an empty gas tank has placed on you. Good!

What's next? The school bus must have been early. As you drive your child to school, you determine exactly what you will say to those school administrators to make sure they know how inconvenienced you are. Your child was "on time" to the bus stop. How dare they send that bus early!

And on it goes. Throughout the day with each little kink, you put on your blame cap and decide who will be next to incur your disapproval.

All the while, you think you are doing great! You are solving problems one-at-a-time, staying on track as best you can, meeting obligations, and maintaining your organized schedule.

But are you? What potential hazard have you overlooked? Is your carefully structured life schedule in danger of imploding?

Of course it is! You might be right on track in keeping control over everything, but you are leaving your peace of mind, self-control, and possibly relationships in the dust. Your attitude is to *"blame and complain,"* then fix the problem. Plus, you are setting a bad example for others and possibly damaging your Christian testimony.

What is a better way to handle those daily interruptions that come along? They always arrive when we have the least time and patience to deal with them, and as a result, we may be negatively affecting others and ourselves by the way we react to them.

Psalm 145:8
"The Lord is gracious, and full of compassion; slow to anger, and of great mercy." (KJV)

God gives us a picture of the right way to handle annoying circumstances. Be slow to anger and show mercy. Even if the school bus schedule changed without your knowledge, what did you accomplish by fussing at the school receptionist? Nothing, except maybe to extract a half-hearted apology. The problem was not resolved by expressing your anger. A better approach would have been to ask for the new bus schedule so that your child would not miss the bus again.

If we allow our human nature to take over, we may tend to get angry first and then try to find a solution. This is opposite of what God wants us to do.

Proverbs 15:1
"A soft answer turneth away wrath: but grievous words stir up anger." (KJV)

Unless you have an absolute saint for a husband, I can almost guarantee that when you phone your husband to blast him for the small amount of gas in the tank, he will yell back at you! What have you accomplished? Instead of making him feel guilty, you fanned the flame of anger.

None of us are perfect. We all have tendencies to say the wrong thing, react the wrong way, or create additional problems instead of finding good solutions.

The next time you are faced with a wrinkle in your daily schedule, try calmly looking for the answer without assigning blame. You will be amazed at the difference in your stress levels, and your family will appreciate your new attitude!

Proverbs 16:32
"He that is slow to anger is better than the mighty…" (KJV)

LF

"Oh, I'm Going To Miss Her"

Christmas time always meant lots of special goodies. The peanut butter balls were my favorite. Mom would buy lots of candy and cookies and fill the house with more calories than any family should eat in a lifetime, not to mention in just a matter of weeks. We would eat our fill. We had no thought of, *"Is this really what I should be eating?"* Oh how good, oh how wonderful!

Someone has said, *"Calories don't count at Christmas."* Is that true? Whether it's true or not, it's a nice way to believe while you are eating your fourteenth peanut butter ball!

One year, my nephew TJ and his mother were the last to leave my parents' house on Christmas Day. Mom told her that she wanted her to take all the candy and junk food that was left to her house because Mom had promised herself that after Christmas, she was going on a diet. Mom had put it off way too long, and over the holidays, she had not thought anything about dieting. Now it was time to get serious.

The first move was to get rid of temptation. TJ saw that Granny was packing up all the goodies and just could not understand what was going on.

So he asked, *"Why is Granny giving us all of her good stuff?"*

His mother told him, *"Granny is going on a diet."*

To that TJ answered, *"Oh, I'm going to miss her."*

If there is something in your life that creates way too much temptation, sack it up, and send it packing! You will be blessed, and God will be pleased. You will be the one to benefit by doing so.

1 Corinthians 10:13
"No temptation has seized you except what is common to man. And God is faithful; he will not let you be tempted beyond what you can bear. But when you are tempted, he will also provide a way out so that you can stand up under it." (NIV)

PS

Mom's Goose is Gone

I just love Canadian geese. I am thrilled when I see them flying over in that beautiful "V" formation. Only God could cause a "not-so-smart" feathered creature to do that. How do they decide who is going to take the lead as they leave the ground and fly? Sometimes there would be 30 of them in one breathtaking V! If men were trying to do that with 30 people, they would be bogged down for days in paperwork trying to decide who gets to be out front.

The geese just get going, and one of them takes the lead. As I read about the geese one day, I discovered that they take turns being in the lead. When the lead goose gets tired, he falls back into the V to rest, and another one takes the lead for a while. It is hard work to be out front all the time.

There is a great lesson here for all of us. Don't stay in the lead too long. Drop back, and let someone else step up to the front.

Even our Lord knew that it was good to *"...Come ye...and rest a while..."* (Mark 6:31 KJV).

Mom loved the look of those Canadian geese that were not real but which made you look twice to see whether or not they were. Everyone seemed to be getting them for their yards. Mom had asked for these for a birthday gift. She was so happy when she unwrapped a pair of beautiful fake geese. The head of one goose was up looking around while the other had his head down in an eating position. I guess as far as fake geese went, these looked ok.

These geese became a permanent fixture in the front yard. The only time they were moved was to mow the grass under their feet. Occasionally though, Mom would have us move them to a new location for a while. But it was for sure and certain that they were not going anywhere on their own.

One day I drove into the front yard and saw that one of the geese was gone. I wondered to myself why Mom would separate this *made-to-be-*

together-for-life pair? Inside, I asked Mom what she had done with the other goose.

She replied, *"nothing, why?"*

I said, *"Well, there is only one out there."*

And with that, she tore out of the house and into the front yard. She was on a mission. Someone had stolen her goose. Where, oh where could it be! Talk about a mad woman! You've probably heard the term, "mad, wet, *settin'* hen?" Maybe some of you have, and others don't have a clue. Well, just hang on; you will get the picture.

You would think that my mom was covered with feathers and would take flight at any moment in order to find her missing baby! But she wasn't and couldn't. We thought that maybe some children in the neighborhood were just having some fun and had taken the goose. We also thought that when they were finished, they would have thrown it in the ditch or maybe put it in someone else's yard.

I drove around for an hour just looking for one lone goose. No luck! I really dreaded going back into that house and telling Mom I couldn't find her missing goose, but I did.

She said to me, *"Call the sheriff."*

I said, *"Mom, you have got to be kidding."* She wasn't, and like the obedient daughter that I was, I called.

I just know that to this day the man who answered the phone still tells his friends about this weird conversation.

"Hello?"

"Hello, I would like to report that one of my mom's geese has been stolen."

"Your mom's what?"

"Her goose. There were two, and now there is only one."

"What does it look like?"

"It's a Canadian goose, and it looks like all the others. It's fake so it had to be stolen because it couldn't move on its own."

I know that I heard that man snickering; no, he was just plain laughing! Well, they had not seen my mom's goose, and they were not much help. I had done what my mom had asked me to do, and that was good enough.

The next day, I went back to her house, and lo-and-behold, the goose was back! How did it get back? We had no idea. Did my mom pray it back? Did word get out in the neighborhood that Mrs. Reynolds was on the warpath about her missing goose and that someone was going to pay? Whatever the reason, the goose was back, and I was glad. On its return, my mom's anger toward the phantom goose thief vanished like a cloud.

Learn a lesson from the goose. Let someone help you in life. You will accomplish more in a shorter amount of time and not be stressed from being overworked.

And do not be like the geese that are lawn decorations. Get up and move! Do not wait for someone to carry you away.

Matthew 11:28
"Come unto me, all ye that labour and are heavy laden, and I will give you rest." (KJV)

Galatians 6:2
"Carry each other's burdens, and in this way you will fulfill the law of Christ." (NIV)

Ephesians 4:32
"And be ye kind one to another, tenderhearted, forgiving one another, even as God for Christ's sake hath forgiven you." (KJV)

PS

Spiritual Giggles

Not Mama Called

Brian was a five-year-old live wire, all boy. Every year of his life was an adventure. Today at age 29, his life is still adventurous to watch from where we are sitting. As parents, we have pretty much a front-row seat. I can honestly say that the *terrible twos* never happened. We set rules, and he followed them. He was not perfect though; after all, he was just a little boy.

I was excited thinking about the day when God would speak to his heart and he would accept the Lord Jesus Christ as his personal Savior. I often wondered how and when it would happen. After all, of all the decisions that the child would make in his life, this was the one that really mattered the most.

An evangelistic team came to our church and held a weeklong revival. The team took care of the music, the message, and even provided a children's service each night. When a child would receive Christ into their hearts, the workers would come into the sanctuary and go quietly to the parents. They would take them to where their son or daughter was so that they might take part in that most precious occasion.

One night I had a strong feeling in my heart that this just might be the night that Brian would trust Jesus as his Savior. During the invitation at the close of the service, I saw one of the young workers head straight to where Guy and I were sitting. My heart was pounding because I just knew she was going to tell us the good news about Brian's salvation. I had already started praising and thanking the Lord for this good news.

As she got to us, all she got out was *"Brian has,"* and I interrupted her by saying, *"I know! He got saved."*

She said, *"No. He threw up!"*

Romans 10:9-10 and 13
"That if thou shalt confess with thy mouth the Lord Jesus, and shalt believe in thine heart that God hath raised him from the dead, thou shalt

be saved. For with the heart man believeth unto righteousness; and with the mouth confession is made unto salvation...For whosoever shall call upon the name of the Lord shall be saved." (KJV)

Yes, *"shall be saved"* by God in His time and not called to salvation by Mama. Moms, pray for your children's salvation. It is the most important thing you can ever do for your child. You should pray like it is all up to you, but trust the Lord, knowing that it is in His hands and will be in His time.

When Brian finally made that life-changing decision to accept Jesus as his personal Savior at age 12, it was in the middle of the night in our living room, just he and his dad. I was in the bed sound asleep. God didn't need me after all.

PS

Washing Away My Sins!

"*H*urry up, we're going to be late for church! Get out of that bed and get moving. Your mom has your breakfast ready. We are going to be late.*"* Every Sunday morning, that was the routine at the Harris household. Everyone knew that Dad would bark the orders, and they would be on time for church in spite of the confusion.

One morning Felicia had just about had it with her little girl. She had been to the bathroom door three times to tell her to hurry up and get finished and that they were going to be late. The shower was running full blast, and Felicia could take it no longer. She knew that Kristen had not been on this earth long enough to be that dirty! She threw the bathroom door open, flung back the shower curtain, and said, *"Kristen, what are you doing!"*

Kristen was holding the hand-held shower and spraying water up and down the walls of the shower. Kristen said, *"I'm washing my sins away!"*

Kristen, the washing has already been done. It's not up to us. Jesus took care of all our cleansing at Calvary. So get out of the shower, dry off, and get going. When you get dirty, call on His name and get clean.

Acts 22:16
"And now why tarriest thou? arise, and be baptized, and wash away thy sins, calling on the name of the Lord." (KJV)

PS

"Where'd Ya Get the Rocks?"

The trip through the mountains on our way to Gatlinburg and Pigeon Forge was wonderful. My sister-in-law and her husband were so impressed with the beauty of it all. Being from Northwest Florida, the mountains were especially breathtaking to them. Marie was carried away by the streams, which would narrow to almost nothing, and then before your eyes, widen to a spectacle of roaring white water rapids over rocks of every size and shape.

Marie and I are artistic gardeners. We love rocks and pieces of old, dead, twisted wood that only nature can make to accent our gardens. Marie is an artist with dirt and flowers. She is head of the Garden Club in her hometown of DeFuniak Springs and has been for years. She has won the *Golden Shovel* award for the last I-don't-know-how-many years.

When she saw these rocks that were worn smooth by years and years of running water, she had to have some. We proceeded to gather and carry some of those beautiful rocks to her van.

A few days later, we stopped by a garden center to shop for trees and flowers. Who, but this woman, would shop for plants while on a vacation? When she made her selections, a very nice young man helped her carry her purchases to the van. Marie opened the door, and there they were as big as Christmas: the rocks.

The young man said, *"Where'd ya get the rocks?"*

Marie was so excited to be able to tell him. She said, *"Oh, the creeks around here are just full of them. You should go and get yourself some."*

With that, the young man looked at Marie and then at me. With a grin that I haven't forgotten to this day and never will, he said, *"You know that it's against the law to take any of those rocks!"*

Oh, my goodness! We were criminals! I have never seen a person close a van door any faster than Marie did that day.

We looked at one another and said, *"What do we do? Do we take them back to the creek?"*

We decided that if we were caught with these rocks in our hands carrying them back to the creek, no one would believe that we were putting them back. Would you? So we shut the door and didn't open that side of the van again until those rocks were safely nested in our gardens.

She made me take some of the rocks so that if we were ever caught, we could do our jail time together. Well, now you can look at me and call me a thief. However, I didn't know at the time that it was against the "rules" to take those rocks!

In today's world with all the means of communication, will anyone be able to say in the end, *"I did not know the rule"*?

The rules are: *You must be born again. The punishment for sin is death. Jesus died for your sins, and the payment for your sin was made at Calvary. You must confess yourself a lost sinner. You must believe in your heart that Jesus died, was buried, and that He rose again and now lives at the right hand of the Father in Heaven.*

Now that you have read this, *you do know the rules.* Make sure that you are grounded in and living for the "Rock of Ages."

Psalm 18:46
"The Lord liveth; and blessed be my rock; and let the God of my salvation be exalted." (KJV)

Psalm 19:14
"May the words of my mouth and the meditation of my heart be pleasing in your sight, O Lord, my Rock and my Redeemer." (NIV)

PS

Wear Your Tiara in the Garden

Yes, I admit it. At times, I am spoiled rotten. My husband frequently states that he spoils me, and that is probably true. He willingly helps in the house, takes care of me, supports my dreams, and encourages my projects. He is always waiting to see what I will do next! I think I add a little spice to his life.

One year while on vacation at the beach, he bought me a T-shirt that was embroidered with the words "Spoiled Rotten." Dave got a lot of mileage out of that T-shirt and was able to roll his eyes with that *"I'm a saint"* look on his face every time someone mentioned it. Actually, it makes him feel proud to know he takes good care of his family.

I am also a Princess. Not because Dave treats me like one (although he does). I am a Princess because of my relationship with God.

It is very simple. My God is the King of Kings, and I am His child. That makes me a Princess! How wonderful to know that it pleases God to take care of His children, and He delights in them.

I will gratefully and happily put on my Tiara and stroll through the Garden of God's forgiveness, provision, mercy, and grace. He showers me with blessings and covers me with His love.

Isaiah 43:15
"I am the Lord...your King." (KJV)

Galatians 3:26
"For ye are all the children of God by faith in Christ Jesus." (KJV)

LF

How Fast is Dark?

When my son Todd was in grade school, we would sit at the kitchen table together and go over his homework, not so much to make sure he had done the assignment or had the right answers, but so that I could keep track of the things he was learning and being taught in school.

I became an expert on science projects, even though they were certainly not my favorite and I cringed at the thought of doing them. One evening Todd was completing his science project on the solar system. We used wire coat hangers to create a revolving mobile and attached painted Styrofoam balls to resemble the various planets.

He wrote a report on his project and included information on each planet and a few lines about space and the speed of light. As he finished the report, Todd said, *"Mom, how fast is the speed of dark? I know how fast the speed of light is."*

Amazed at his inquisitive mind, I found myself floundering for an answer. As a mother, I was supposed to have all the answers, right? I could not let him know that I had no clue how fast the speed of dark was. Who ever asked a question like that!

After stammering around, trying to act as if I knew what I was talking about, I said, *"Son, let's just finish this project first, and then we can talk about the speed of dark."*

It was a flimsy attempt to take his mind off the question. The truth was that I did not have an answer.

Dr. Clay Nuttall, a professor at Piedmont Baptist College and my Bible Study Hour teacher, always states, *"What Does the Text Say,"* when he is teaching our class.

What does God say about darkness? How fast is it? How long does it last?

1 Samuel 2:9
"...but the wicked will be silenced in darkness." (NIV)

Job 12:25
"They grope in darkness with no light..." (NIV)

These passages sound ominous, and I know that the darkness is a place I do not want to be.

Proverbs 4:19
"But the way of the wicked is like deep darkness; they do not know what makes them stumble." (NIV)

God uses the word darkness to describe circumstances where sin has entered your life, and you are trying to find a way out. It is a picture of a soul without Christ and one who is doomed to an eternity without Him.

Have you ever been unable to fall asleep at night? You lie there, watching the clock, wishing you could sleep, becoming more frustrated as the moments tick by. The night seems to last forever. Your mind will not "shut up." Your thoughts tumble over each other, and you try everything, but sleep does not come.

How fast is darkness? Once it arrives, it can seem like an eternity. If you allow yourself to enter into the darkness of sin, it can be a slow process to escape. The darkness does not pass quickly.

Ecclesiastes 5:17
"All his days he eats in darkness, with great frustration, affliction and anger." (NIV)

Once darkness takes hold in your life, it eats at you, digs deep into you, and will not let go.

Darkness can also be circumstances and situations that result in illness, depression, grief, or loneliness. Darkness can represent the life of someone who has turned away from God or fallen into despair.

How do we escape it? Of course, resisting temptation to sin would be ideal. But we are human, and often times we make bad choices that lead to darkness in our hearts and lives. We find ourselves captured, trapped, and it envelopes us like darkness descending at night.

There is only one escape from this, and the answer is the Lord Jesus Christ.

Micah 7:8
"...Though I have fallen, I will rise. Though I sit in darkness, the Lord will be my light." (NIV)

John 12:46
"I have come into the world as a light, so that no one who believes in me should stay in darkness." (NIV)

God provided a way of escape. His mercy, forgiveness, and grace are larger than any sin, any darkness.

Psalm 18:28
"...my God turns my darkness into light." (NIV)

Psalm 107:14
"He brought them out of darkness...and broke away their chains." (NIV)

How fast is the dark? Fast enough to cause you to walk into it with your eyes wide-open. Darkness can descend in a moment but take a lifetime to overcome.

Todd, I know that someday you will be on the receiving end of some of those deep questions as your own sons, Zachary and Jackson, grow up. I want to be there when they do!

LF

Stop, Drop, and Roll

We were all taught the Stop, Drop, and Roll procedure when we were children. This is the method to use if your clothes are on fire. We were shown how to drop to the ground and roll around to put out the flames.

Naturally, I wanted to make sure that Zachary knew about this life-saving procedure.

One day I asked Zachary, *"What would you do if your clothes were on fire?"*

He quickly responded, *"Nana, I just wouldn't put them on!"* Out of the mouths of babes!

As a child in grade school, my friends and I had great fun rolling around in the grass pretending our dresses were on fire. The teacher made a game out of it. We would start running across the playground and listen for her call to *"Stop."*

At that moment, we knew we were to stop running, fall on the grass, and start rolling from side to side to extinguish the pretend fire.

The purpose of this exercise was to make sure that we knew exactly what to do in the event of a fire. We heard it, and we practiced it. Even to this day, when I hear the words, *"Stop, Drop, and Roll,"* I immediately know exactly what it means and what I am supposed to do.

Did you know that God also has a Stop, Drop, and Roll procedure in place for His children? Usually, when fire erupts in our lives, we tend to RUN! We may be caught off-guard by it, or we may run because we do not know what to do.

Sometimes we run away out of guilt or shame, knowing that we started the fire in the first place. Other times we did not start the fire but saw it burning and did nothing to stop it. We just continued down the same destructive path we were on and did nothing to alter our course or change our ways.

Indeed, the fire in our life may be caused by something completely out of our control. The situation burst into flames, and we were suddenly caught up in it unintentionally.

However the fire starts, God has a perfect plan already in place to help you extinguish it.

Step 1 is **STOP**.

Exodus 14:13
"And Moses said unto the people, Fear ye not, stand still, and see the salvation of the Lord…" (KJV)

Moses had led the children of Israel out of Egypt, and now Pharaoh's army was chasing them. They were stopped at the Red Sea with no apparent way of escape. The "fire" they were experiencing was red hot, and God commanded them to stand still.

Another example of this is found in Numbers 9:8.

Numbers 9:8
"And Moses said unto them, Stand still, and I will hear what the Lord will command concerning you." (KJV)

In this situation, the people were confused at the celebration of Passover and needed guidance and direction as to what was clean and acceptable and what was unclean and defiled.

1 Samuel 12:7
"Now therefore stand still, that I may reason with you before the Lord…" (KJV)

The people had sinned and forsaken God. Once again, God stepped in to bring about a change and provide direction and salvation.

God's Word is full of examples on standing still. Wonder why He has to tell us multiple times? Perhaps this instruction is so important that He wants to make sure we get the message!

Is that any different from you? Those of you with children know exactly what I mean. You do not tell a child something one time and expect that child to do it the first time or remember it the next time. Sometimes you have to tell the child many, many times in order for them to comprehend and obey.

Remember, if you run around, you will only "fan the flames." So the first step in putting out the fire in your life is to **STOP**.

Step 2 is **DROP**.

Psalm 95:6
"Come, let us bow down in worship, let us kneel before the Lord our maker." (NIV)

Psalm 102:17
"He will respond to the prayer of the destitute…" (NIV)

Matthew 21:22
"And all things, whatsoever ye shall ask in prayer, believing, ye shall receive." (KJV)

Drop to your knees and pray. God delights in the prayers of His children and will not leave you alone to put out the fire in your life. He will hear you and answer you. His answer may not always be the answer you want, but His answers will certainly be what He knows is best for you. Sometimes *NO* answer *IS* the answer.

Many times I have heard bitter people complaining that they prayed to God, but He did not answer them. My question to those people is: Did you tell God what you wanted Him to do for you, or did you seek His will in the situation? How are you praying? Are you honoring God with your prayer, or are you making demands?

Step 3 is **ROLL.**

God will give you everything you need to deal with the fire in your life. It may be strength and fortitude, it may be opportunity, and it may even be through the intervention of another person.

It is up to you to roll with the punches and use the armor of God to sustain you through to the end.

And remember, like Zachary said, don't put on those burning clothes to start with, and you can avoid the fire.

Ephesians 6:11
"Put on the whole armour of God, that ye may be able to stand…" (KJV)

LF

The Greatest Gardener

in the World

My husband Guy is one of the best gardeners in the world. When we moved into our home in 1972, one of the first things he did was to clear away big rocks and make room for the garden.

Guy believes in mulch. Every blade of grass he has cut over the years has been put either into the vegetable garden or the flower gardens. Every leaf that has fallen in our yard has been gathered and put into the vegetable garden. Every vegetable peeling, every tea bag, every coffee ground has, you guessed it, been put into the garden. You talk about good dirt – we've got it!

We work on the flower gardens together. I love clipping all the spent flowers. I know that if I get rid of the old, then new ones will come, usually bigger and better. I like seeing something I have planted multiply and reproduce. I also love talking to the Lord as I work.

Do you know that if you are out in your yard with a shovel, hoe, wheel barrel, watering hose, and clippers, looking and smelling like yesterday's dirty socks, then nobody will come near you? Either they usually can't stand the smell, or they know you might just put them to work.

So most of the time, it is just God and me. What sweet fellowship. What a time for praising Him. I am reminded of His perfection when I see one of my beautiful soft pink roses, looking like they should be decorating a birthday cake. The smell! Oh, how wonderful!

If you have never smelled a rose from the garden, you have missed a blessing. The florist greenhouse can create the beauty, but the perfection comes only when the smell compliments it, and only God's hand brings that. When man forces plants to grow in a hot house, fast and furiously, the aroma of God's creation is lost. Man can come close, but only God can create perfection.

As I look at that perfectly beautiful, wonderfully smelling rose as it ages and withers away, I am reminded of loved ones who have gone on, making way for the next generation to stand out and be noticed. I am further reminded of how God could withhold the much-needed sunshine and rain, but He doesn't. He gives us what we need when we need it.

1 Peter 1:23-25

"Being born again, not of corruptible seed, but of incorruptible, by the word of God, which liveth and abideth for ever. For all flesh is as grass, and all the glory of man as the flower of grass. The grass withereth, and the flower thereof falleth away: But the word of the Lord endureth for ever. And this is the word which by the gospel is preached unto you." (KJV)

One of the first acts of Creation was the garden, and what a garden it must have been. There He walked and talked with a man. In Genesis, the Bible says that every tree and every herb needed by man was in the garden. Man is still able to get everything he needs from the garden. Vegetable gardens provide food, and oh how good those fresh-from-the-garden groceries are.

One of the greatest miracles ever performed was in the garden. While on His knees in the garden, Jesus met with His Heavenly Father. He met with His enemy, who pretended to be His friend, as he betrayed Him in the garden. The end result of this betrayal was a cruel and horrible death on a cross (John 19:41).

Jesus went to the garden many times throughout His earthly ministry. He walked in the garden, He fellowshipped with and ministered to His friends in the garden, and there He was betrayed. There also He rose from the dead, conquering death for all mankind and completing salvation's plan.

There at the empty tomb after His resurrection, He was mistaken for the gardener (John 20:15). Surely He was, and still is, the greatest gardener this world has ever known. He began it all in a perfect garden. When He comes again, He will bring perfection that will last throughout all eternity.

Revelation 21:4-5

"And God shall wipe away all tears from their eyes; and there shall be no more death, neither sorrow, nor crying, neither shall there be any more pain: for the former things are passed away. And he that sat upon the throne said, Behold, I make all things new. And he said unto me, Write: for these words are true and faithful." (KJV)

PS

Sorry is the Wrong Word

People use the word "sorry" millions of times per day around the world! The word used to stand for regret for something done wrong. Today the word is over-used and continually misused in our daily conversations. Saying we are sorry for something we actually did *wrong* is at the bottom of the list of reasons why people use the word.

I recently attended an awards meeting. The manager announced the annual top performers and called them by name. Upon hearing her name called, one woman stood up and said, *"Sorry,"* to the people sitting at her table and then sat back down. It was as if she was apologizing for the inconvenience of other people having to hear about her success or apologizing because she won and they did not.

We use the word "sorry" instead of saying "pardon me" if we did not hear or understand fully what someone said.

We say "sorry" and begin to explain again if someone said "sorry" while we were speaking.

We use the word "sorry" instead of "excuse me" if we accidentally bump into someone. We also say "sorry" if someone bumps into us!

We use the word "sorry" to apologize for someone else's actions. Parents are really good at this.

We say "sorry" if someone else makes a mistake, as in *"Sorry, you have the wrong number."* Why are we apologizing?

We say "sorry" when we step into an elevator and another person moves over to make room. Why not just say, "thank you"?

We say, *"Sorry, I should have thought of that before,"* when making a suggestion. Since when did having a good idea mean that you have to apologize for not having the idea sooner?

We say we feel "sorry" for someone. This probably means we sympathize or have empathy for another person.

In fact, we use "sorry" for everything from expressing grief to joy, regret to forgiveness, mistakes to accomplishments.

Pamela Delgado, a dear co-worker and Christian friend, told me that when she was growing up, her father forbade her from using the phrase "I'm sorry."

She explained that the word "sorry" carried an extremely negative and judgmental definition in their culture. Stereotypical examples of the word "sorry" in the Native American culture could express an opinion that an individual is worthless, lazy, or has a poor work ethic.

What does God say about the word "sorry"? I found that the word is used to describe a state of repentance. God expects us to repent of our sins and turn from them.

I am sorry, but I am concerned that God's true meaning of the word is diluted by the misguided way it is currently used.

Sorry, but I believe we should say what we mean. If we did something wrong, we should apologize. There are a multitude of other words we can use to express the right meaning and feeling for all the other situations.

Sorry, but sometimes God puts something on my heart, and I just have to write it down.

Psalm 38:18
"...I will be sorry for my sin." (KJV)

2 Corinthians 7:10
"Godly sorrow brings repentance that leads to salvation and leaves no regret..." (NIV)

LF

Don't You Just Love the Garden?

Most people think of a garden in one of two ways: a flower garden or a vegetable garden. In our minds we envision ladies with wide-brimmed straw hats resting under shade trees, sipping sweet iced tea, and admiring the colorful flowers and foliage. We see a gardener taking great care to plant those vegetables, pull the weeds, water and cultivate the soil, and finally enjoy the harvest.

God provides examples of His gardens in the Bible, and it is worth taking a peek to understand the importance He places on the garden experience.

God's garden is a <u>prepared place.</u>

Genesis 2:8-9
"Now the Lord God had planted a garden in the east, in Eden...And the Lord God made all kinds of trees grow out of the ground – trees that were pleasing to the eye and good for food. In the middle of the garden were the tree of life and the tree of the knowledge of good and evil." (NIV)

God's love is so great He prepared a perfect garden for His children. This is a glorious picture of the preparations He is making for our home in the garden of heaven.

God's garden is a <u>cultivated place</u> with plenty of water and sunshine.

Job 8:16
"He is like a well-watered plant in the sunshine, spreading its shoots over the garden." (NIV)

Every aspect of the garden was carefully designed to provide the water, the sunshine, and to remove anything detrimental to the growth of the garden.

God's garden is a place of celebration.

Esther 1:5
"When these days were over, the king gave a banquet, lasting seven days, in the enclosed garden of the king's palace, for all the people from the least to the greatest..." (NIV)

How delightful! God expects His people to enjoy the garden.
I recently attended a bridal shower in Phyllis' garden. It was a down-home celebration indeed, and all the ladies wore hats! We loved being in the garden and spent hours in fellowship and fun!

God's garden is a place of beauty.

Ezekiel 28:13
"Thou hast been in Eden the garden of God; every precious stone was thy covering, the sardius, topaz, and the diamond, the beryl, the onyx, and the jasper, the sapphire, the emerald, and the carbuncle, and gold..." (KJV)

It was not an accident that God designed gardens to surround us with nature's more glorious array of color. He wants beauty in our lives.

God's garden is a place of knowledge.

Genesis 2:9
"...In the middle of the garden were the tree of life and the tree of the knowledge of good and evil." (NIV)

God does not expect us to go through life ignorant. He provides opportunities for us to learn and grow in the garden as we study His Word.

God's garden is a <u>picture of love.</u>

Song of Songs 4:12
"You are a garden locked up, my sister, my bride; you are a spring enclosed, a sealed fountain." (NIV)

Song of Songs 6:2
"My lover has gone down to his garden, to the beds of spices, to browse in the gardens and to gather lilies." (NIV)

God used a garden to illustrate the passion and beauty of love and the pleasure found in the love relationship.

God's garden is a <u>place of prayer.</u>

John 18:1
"When Jesus had spoken these words, he went forth with his disciples over the brook Ce'dron, where was a garden, into the which he entered, and his disciples." (KJV)

Luke 22:40-41
"And when he was at the place...he was withdrawn...and kneeled down, and prayed." (KJV)

Do you go to the garden of prayer and seek God's will for your life? Jesus found comfort in prayer in the garden.

God's garden is a <u>place of escape.</u>

Jeremiah 39:4
"...they fled; they left the city at night by way of the king's garden, through the gate..." (NIV)

God always provides a means of escape. He does not allow us to be over-burdened without providing the strength and knowledge to deal with the situations.

God's garden is a <u>picture of eternal life</u>.

John 19:41
"At the place where Jesus was crucified, there was a garden, and in the garden a new tomb, in which no one had ever been laid." (NIV)

Yes, Jesus died and was buried in the garden. But the story did not end there. It was only the beginning.

Luke 24:5-6
"...Why seek ye the living among the dead? He is not here, but is risen..." (KJV)

Hallelujah! Glory to God! He arose in the garden! And He has given us a thrilling picture of resurrection, power, and eternal life!

Don't you just love the garden? What has He done for you in your garden of life?

LF

Service Giggles

Notebooks and Blueberry Muffins

Miss Little, my English teacher, told me that I should write. I have tried my best to forget what she said to me that day in class. I have been unsuccessful in forgetting. Maybe she was right; we will see.

It was 10:00 a.m., and we were on vacation in Florida. That was the day that I began to do what Miss Little was so sure that I could do. My husband had just dragged himself out of bed.

As he made his way over to where I was sitting, he said, *"What are you doing?"*

I said, *"I am writing a book."* I thought to myself, *"I hope this will be a best seller so I can knock that look right off of his face!"*

"OK, Lord, I surrender!" In 1992, I gave up and went to college at the young age of 45. That day on vacation in Florida, I gave up and began to write. I ran from college for 27 years. I now have a degree in music. It was the hardest thing, I do believe, I have ever done in my life.

Can you even imagine having a Senior Voice recital with 18 "art songs" from memory at the ripe old age of 49? That was no laughing matter, and believe me, I was not laughing. But with God's help, I finished it, and I have the degree!

I had been running from "the book" for only three years. I was learning faster, or else I was just too old to keep running.

I am always amazed at how God speaks to His children to move them in the direction He has for them. I have learned through the years to listen for His voice in the most unlikely places and situations. I think the more unusual the situation, the clearer His voice becomes.

My husband Guy and our son Brian are die-hard Gator fans. On our way to South Florida, we stopped by the University of Florida campus. We enjoy going to their bookstore. While I was there, I heard God's voice loud and clear—God's voice speaking to me through an enormous stack of three-subject, spiral-bound notebooks on sale for 49 cents. They were leftover notebooks from the University of Florida School of Law, School of Medicine, School of Dentistry, School of Nursing, and the School of Business.

None of those subjects were any of my business! Did I tell you that the price was only 49 cents? I live to find bargains. I have a real hard time passing up an unbelievable price of any kind. It does not matter if it does not fit, if I like it or not, if I need it or not, or if I have plenty of it already. All that matters is the bargain!

I heard the voice inside of me say, *"You need to use these notebooks to begin writing the book while you are on vacation."* I walked around the three-foot stack of notebooks more than six times. I would pick up one of the notebooks and then put it down. I kept thinking that I would look silly buying any one of these notebooks. They were none of my business.

Besides, Brian and Guy would be sure to say, *"What did you buy that for?"* I just hate it when husbands and sons ask questions you just do not want to answer! I said *"no"* to the cheap, unbelievable bargain notebooks, not to mention to the voice inside of me.

I heard the voice telling me to buy the notebooks on Saturday. I heard the voice over and over again as the week went on. I saw the stack of notebooks in my mind a thousand times. I knew that I should have just bought the notebooks!

Later that week, I went to the grocery store to get eggs and milk for blueberry muffins. As I turned down the produce aisle, heading for the eggs, the voice spoke to me once again, louder and clearer. God put me face to face with NOTEBOOKS, spiral bound, three subjects! 49 cents? NO! They were $1.49!

I had missed a bargain by not listening to the voice. I was not about to miss a blessing. I bought the notebook! Who in the world but God would have ever put the notebooks in the produce department?

I hope you will enjoy the "book" as much as Guy and Brian enjoyed the blueberry muffins.

God speaks to His children in such wonderful ways as we walk with Him. Moses listened to Him through the burning bush; Baleem listened to Him through the voice of a donkey; and I listened to Him through notebooks and blueberry muffins.

John 10:4

"...he goeth before them, and the sheep follow him: for they know his voice." (KJV)

PS

I Am Sitting Up Straight in My Seat

God called me to go back to school when I was 45 years old. I had been out of high school for 27 years.

The admission counselor at Piedmont Baptist College told me that I had to take the SAT test.

I said, *"You have got to be kidding!"*

He wasn't. He told me, however, that it didn't matter what I made on the test, but it had to be in my admission file. Now let me tell you, that doesn't make any sense to me. Why take a test if the score doesn't matter? I did not want to take that test. There are no words that can tell you just how much I did not want to take it.

I was told to go to Parkland High School, and there I would be able to get a study manual. I did and found out that the test was going to be in just a few days. I was just "under the wire" to register to take the test. I had no time to study the study guide. Would it have made a difference? Who knows? I was a miserable person as I waited for the test date to arrive.

The Friday night before the test on Saturday, I got on my knees in my bathroom (hugging the "throne," which was clean of course) and cried my eyes out. I told God that it was all right with me if He had changed His mind about me going to school, that I would understand, and that it would be all right with me.

He just had to help me. I longed for the peace of His will. Feeling scared, dumb, and pretty much defeated, I was just getting started, and He had to help me.

Finally, I told Him that I knew He was calling me to school, but I didn't know why. The need to know why was up to Him to tell me later.

I said, *"Lord, I'm going to bed now and sleep."* That was the one thing I knew I could do. I set my alarm clock, and the next morning I reported to Reynolds High School to take the test. The rest and the results were up to Him.

The next morning I was in line with kids who looked at me with looks on their faces that said, *"Who in the world are you, and why are you in this line?"* I did have the clearest skin in the bunch! My clothes were the only clothes in the room that had been ironed. I had my paper in hand, and it was none of their business what was going on between the Lord and me.

The teacher was a full-grown adult, and I was sure to get a reassuring smile from him. I didn't. I took my seat. Each section of the test took 30 minutes. I had read in the study guide that if you were not sure of an answer, not to answer. During each section of the test, answers that I was sure of only took me about five minutes. I colored in the dots so carefully. I tried to take as long on each one as I possibly could.

I spent the other 25 minutes talking to the Lord and pretending that I was coloring in some more dots. All the kids in that room were so busy! They all seemed to be so smart; it broke my heart for me. I will never forget the feeling that was going through me at the time. I can truly say that God was more real to me during that test than I could have imagined. Our fellowship was sweet. I was praying that I could be reassured of His presence and His promise that He would never leave me (Hebrews 13:5).

All of a sudden, I heard ZZZZZZZZZZ (snoring) behind me. I looked over my shoulder, and what do you know? This great big football-player-type figure of a teenage boy was falling out of his seat sound asleep!

Praise the Lord! I began sitting up straight in my seat, realizing that I might not be the dumbest person in the room!

God sent a smile just when I needed it most! Although I had a quiet smile on the outside, on the inside it was a full-blown giggle.

And would you believe it! I graduated in four years with honors! To God be the glory! Great things He has done!

Nehemiah 8:10
"...the joy of the Lord is your strength." (KJV)

2 Timothy 4:7
"I have fought a good fight, I have finished my course, I have kept the faith." (KJV)   PS

Throw Your Net

God Will Take Care of the Catch!

How many ladies would just love to hear their husband say, *"Honey, we're going fishing. Get the cooler, get your poles, get your knife for cleaning and scaling, and we will catch a good mess of fish for you to cook up. We are going to have a time in this world!"*

Now, I know there are ladies that like that sort of outing with their husbands, but not me! No, sir. I cannot stand to fish. I cannot bare the fact that I cannot see what is going on under that water. Where are the fish? Are they getting ready to take my bait and get on my hook? Are they going to someone else's line? Are they swimming in the area? What kind of "fish food" do they want? Are they all lying on the bottom of the lake laughing at me?

People like me want to go, get it done, and get on with what's next. I am a hyperactive person, and sitting and fishing is just too slow for me. I am a "3-B" kind of fisherman – Broiled, Baked, or Blackened! My favorite fishing hole is the Red Lobster.

It takes a lot of patience and faith to be a fisherman. Do you suppose that is the reason Jesus chose so many of the disciples from the fishing profession? Matthew 4:19 (KJV) tells us that Jesus, seeing Simon and Andrew, called to them and said, *"...Follow me, and I will make you fishers of men."*

Fishing for men is a lot like fishing for fish; it takes time, patience, perseverance, faith, equipment, and the right location. The scriptures always talk about the fishermen casting their nets. Never do you read that they fished with poles. I would much prefer to net fish than pole fish; at least you could catch more than one at a time.

Are you willing to be a fisher of men? Are you willing to do whatever it takes and fish for the souls of men as we are commanded in the scriptures? Well then, throw the net; God will take care of the catch! Throwing the net might be as simple as inviting a neighbor to church. After church, feed them Sunday dinner. Dinner tables are a great place to fish. That is called faith fishing. You are only responsible before God to throw the net, and He will take care of the catch.

Matthew 4:19
"...Follow me, and I will make you fishers of men." (KJV)

PS

Fishing With a Clean Net

Luke Chapter 5 tells us about two fishermen who had come in from a long and trying fishing trip. They had fished all night and had caught nothing. Even though they had caught nothing, their nets were in need of cleaning and mending for the next day. Men who are serious about catching fish know what it takes: the right equipment that is properly cared for.

God says in His Word that we are to follow Him and He will make us *"fishers of men"* (Matthew 4:19 KJV). When He is ready for you to fish for Him, will you be ready? What kind of net will you throw when you go fishing? Is it dirty? Is it torn? Is it in knots?

Now, you're not going to throw a literal net. Your life, your testimony, your work ethic, your demeanor, your attitude, your reputation before people: that's your net.

What does your net look like, smell like, feel like? Is it full of knots that cannot be untangled? Is it full of holes that are so big that you couldn't possibly catch anything? Is it dirty with things that have piled up in your net, things that should never have gotten in there in the first place?

It's up to each one of us to be aware of who we are and who we belong to. At any time, He could call on us to fish for Him. Will we be ready? Will our net be clean and worthy of use by the Master?

I was scheduled to speak a few months ago at a ladies' meeting. Wouldn't you know that right before the meeting, I got my net really dirty. I had bought three pairs of shoes at a store in the mall. I tried them on in the store but knew that I would try them on again at home to make sure they were what I wanted. I did not like one pair so I took it back to the store.

I had put all three pairs on my charge card (charge cards make for easy returns). They wouldn't credit my card for the returned pair because they were on sale. They would only give me a store credit. I was not a happy shopper, but I held my tongue. I didn't dare let that thing get loose! But my face, eyes, and body gestures were speaking volumes as to how I felt about their store policy. I was really hateful to the lady waiting on me. I took the store credit and snatched that credit slip right out of her hand. Do I even need to tell you that this was not Christ-like?

I was proud of myself that I had let her know in no uncertain terms that I was not happy! I felt like a winner, even though she had my money and all I had was her store credit slip.

A few days later as I was trying to study for my upcoming ladies' meeting, I couldn't think of anything but my so-called "victory." It was giving me indigestion, sleeplessness, depression, you name it; it was not setting well with me. I knew that I was going fishing. There just might be a soul that God needed to draw into His kingdom with my net, and it was dirty, unfit, filthy, and in a very tight knot.

What was I going to do? What would you have done? I marched right into the mall, went right into that store to wash my net. The store was full of people, not what I wanted to see, an audience. I know God has a sense of humor. I felt His smile as He watched me undo what should not have been done in the first place. I was on a mission. I needed to study, and God needed to use me. So I had to do what I needed to do.

The lady who had helped me before was working. She kept running in and out of the back room getting one shoe and then another for her customers. When she made eye contact with me, I went in for a "cleansing."

She said, *"May I help you?"*

I said, *"Sure, but first I have got to make something right. I was in here the other day, and I was rude to you concerning your store policy on returns. I am a Christian, and I didn't act too much like one in front of you. I want you to forgive me."*

She said, *"Sure, no problem."*

That lady was probably as shocked as any person who had just been held up at gunpoint. She made a bullet dash for the back and never made eye contact with me again. She probably thought I was going to start preaching. Well, I left there with another pair of shoes and a clean net! Ready to fish!

Keeping ourselves clean and ready for use by our Lord and Savior isn't always easy. It is always our choice. He has made provisions for our cleansing through His Word and the Holy Spirit.

Matthew 5:23-24
"Therefore, if you are offering your gift at the altar and there remember that your brother has something against you, leave your gift there in front of the altar. First go and be reconciled to your brother; then come and offer your gift." (NIV)

1 John 1:9
"If we confess our sins, he is faithful and just to forgive us our sins, and to cleanse us from all unrighteousness." (KJV)

PS

Open Eyes and a Willing Heart

Women wear a multitude of hats. We have a closet full of them and are experts at picking the perfect hat for the right occasion. We learned at an early age the importance of juggling these hats and never letting one slip through our hands to hit the ground. In other words, we can multi-task.

That brings me to my point. Exactly what is the purpose of all these hats? What is the role of women? In speaking in seminars and conferences over the years, I began to realize that we all have different ideas and thoughts about what women should be doing at certain ages in their lives.

But I have been given a great deal of bad information. Over the years, women have said things to me that gave me a false assumption, such as:

- As you get older, your life will slow down.
- Grow old gracefully. Just sit back, smile and nod, and do not push yourself.
- I taught Sunday School for many years. Now it is time to let the younger women take over.
- I do not have any babies in the nursery so I let the other mothers handle the duty.
- I used to sing in the choir, but now I am going to sit back and just enjoy hearing other people do it.
- I do not have children in the Awana Club or Youth Choir; why should I help?
- I figured it out by myself, with NO help. Let them figure it out too.

After hearing these statements, I came to the wrong conclusion. I thought that, as I grew older, my responsibilities would become lighter. I would have less to do, more free time, and could be the recipient of the hard work of others without investing one moment of my own time to do anything constructive.

WRONG! It is not happening that way in my life. At my age, I am so much more involved, so busy, that I can hardly keep up with it. My life is bursting with activity, and I truly believe I have more to do today than I did when I was 30 years old. Wait a minute! What happened to this rest and relaxation I am supposed to experience?

I wanted to know the truth about what to expect and turned for answers to the primary authority on life. I searched the Bible for what God said about older women and what we should be doing.

The only reference that fit my situation was found in Titus 2:3-5.

Titus 2:3-5
*"Likewise, teach the older women to be reverent in the way they live, not to be slanderers or addicted to much wine, but to teach what is good. Then they can train the younger women to love their husbands and children, to be self-controlled and pure, to be busy at home, to be kind, and to be subject to their husbands, so that no one will malign the word of God." *(NIV)

Let me tell you what I did not find in Titus 2:3-5. Nowhere in my Bible did I find anything, any verse, that told me I should sit down, kick back, and let the younger women do it.

What exactly do those verses mean, and how do they apply to my life today? Let me start by conducting a short exercise. Read the following list, and put a checkmark beside anything that you have personally experienced in your life.

- ☐ House burned to the ground
- ☐ Husband had a brain tumor
- ☐ Chronically ill child
- ☐ Raised children
- ☐ Had trouble with a teenager
- ☐ Primary care of aging parent
- ☐ Friend turned against you
- ☐ Loss of a parent
- ☐ Marriage problems
- ☐ Blended family – stepchildren
- ☐ Financial issues
- ☐ In love/out of love
- ☐ Trouble in the church
- ☐ Trouble with neighbors
- ☐ Personal illness or surgery
- ☐ Illness of a family member
- ☐ Working mother
- ☐ Loss of a job
- ☐ Husband lost his job
- ☐ Taught Sunday School
- ☐ Helped in youth activities
- ☐ Planted a garden – grew weeds
- ☐ Worried about anything
- ☐ Experienced sorrow, grief, or mourning
- ☐ Changed jobs or careers

I am confident that you checked several of these, which means that you can relate to me. This is My List! This is my Life! I have experienced all of these things and much, much more. And I am sure your life has been just as full. This list could go on indefinitely!

I remember my life at age 27. During one year, my husband lost his job, our house burned to the ground, my husband had a brain tumor, and my young daughter became chronically ill. What a year!

What does all this tell us? We live by God's grace, and we are survivors by His mercy. We have experienced some of life's best and some of the very worse, and yet we are still here.

Together, we have a tremendous amount of experience in everything from love, marriage, children, family, church, emotions, intellectual, financial, relationship, intimacy…and so on. We have Been There!

So let's go back to Titus 2:3-5 and determine what that scripture really means. I believe women have a great deal to offer. Every experience, every heartache, every problem, every joy, everything that we have dealt with in our lives has taught or provided us with something, some knowledge or expertise, that we can pass on in order to help another person.

I believe we should use every ounce of energy, every bit of experience, every piece of learning, every emotion, and every source of strength to reach out and help someone.

We did not experience all those life lessons just so we could sit back, check it off the list, and say, *"OK, Lord, got through that one."*

I am not talking about projects. Most of you have probably already been involved in the ladies' organizations at your churches. You have worked on a mission's project, put together a missionary closet, and stitched a quilt or something like that.

What a legacy you can build and what a message you can send to women simply by observing the principle of Titus 2:3-5. You can be the most exciting, motivating woman just by having your eyes open and a willing heart.

LF

Can I Get a Tutu, Please?

When I was growing up, I wanted to take ballet lessons. My dream was to spin and twirl, dance on my toes, and wear a tutu…all that girly stuff. My parents could not afford ballet lessons so it was something I never had the chance to do.

Naturally, when I had my own daughter, I wanted her to have things I never had. You did the same thing with your children, right? So Marci started ballet lessons and tap dancing lessons at the age of four. Every spring, there was a dance recital at Reynolds Auditorium in Winston-Salem.

At each of those recitals, I would position myself as close to the front of the auditorium as I could get. I was so proud, so excited to watch my daughter up on that stage.

Marci had been taking dance lessons for two years, and it was time for the spring recital. The performance began, and the little girls came twirling on the stage. Marci was up there, spinning and tapping and bouncing away with all the other little six year olds.

Smack in the middle of all those little girls was a woman, probably 45 years old, wearing a tutu and leotard and dancing her heart out. She danced, jumped, and tapped her way across that stage along with the children.

People were whispering, saying, *"Look at that old woman up there. Who does she think she is? What is she doing up there?"*

But as the recital progressed, this woman kept appearing, and it became obvious that she was thoroughly engrossed in dancing every step. By the end of the recital, people in the audience were cheering and applauding. I later learned that this woman's life dream had been to take dance lessons. She put aside her fear and got up there! She danced her heart out.

The point is….***Go Ahead and Dance***! Nobody cares if you cannot dance well. No one cares what you look like. Just Do It! Your friends will love you anyway. This woman fulfilled her deepest longing and at the same time set a great example for those little girls.

It is never too late to Dance! It is never too late to follow your heart or follow God's gentle urging to do His will.

Go Ahead and Dance. Dance through your purpose, dreams, and desires. Don't be afraid to try something new. If God gives you the assignment, He will be there to help you accomplish it!

Remember, a lone amateur built the ark. A large group of professionals built the Titanic. I would much rather go through these years of my life dancing my heart out than rocking on the porch as I "grow old gracefully."

Years from now, I want to look back on my life and know that I was able to make a difference in someone else's journey. I want to follow every dream, and live every moment to the fullest.

Who knows! Next year my family may be sitting on the front row of Reynolds Auditorium watching me in a dance recital!

Ecclesiastes 3:1-4
"There is a time for everything, and a season for every activity under heaven: a time to be born and a time to die, a time to plant and a time to uproot, a time to kill and a time to heal, a time to tear down and a time to build, a time to weep and a time to laugh, a time to mourn and a time to dance." (NIV)

LF

40-Plus - What?

What do women want? There are many pre-conceived notions about what women want and need. But what is the real truth about us?

I searched online and found a list written by psychological professionals. The article details specifically what women want at various ages in their lives.

The section that really caught my attention was the list of what women in the 40-plus age group are expecting and what people *believe* about these women. Here is a snapshot of that list.

As a Rule, women age 40 and above:

- Have a greater degree of psychological issues
- Are more depressed than younger women
- Are preoccupied with childhood memories
- Are less satisfied with their lives
- Have a decline in sexual desire and interest
- Are not capable of physical intimacy
- Have fewer social connections
- Focus mainly on keeping the family together
- Are resigned to aging gracefully

Is this truly what people think about us? Personally, I do not want anybody to think those things about me. I do not want to be lumped together in a category that expects me to get old mentally and be satisfied with doing nothing!

Last year, eight couples in my Sunday School Class went to Myrtle Beach for a few days of relaxation. While we were there, all the women went out on the beach and built a cheerleading pyramid! Can you just picture eight middle-aged women doing that! What a sight we must have been! Phyllis even paid a young boy to make pictures of us (she called it a "tip")!

That is priceless! Do you think these eight women would be content to sit in a chair and isolate themselves from life? Not at all. I am not ready to sit down, grow old gracefully, and do nothing for God or anyone else.

So what do you want? Are there things you always wanted to do that you never did, probably because you were busy raising child, taking care of your home, and working a job? Did you put your desires and purpose on the backburner in order to take care of life's responsibilities?

I, like many of you, did the same thing. I focused on raising my children, being involved in every aspect of their lives, being a hands-on mother (even when they did not want me to be hands-on). And I focused on making a living and working a full-time job.

As my children grew up, I realized that there were many things I had put aside, things I had determined years earlier that I wanted to do with my life. There were things that I knew God had called me to do, or prepared me to do, but I was so busy with daily life that I did not do them.

I spent a large amount of time thinking about these things and made up my mind to go ahead and pursue my dreams. What I learned was that God had a plan for my life, and He instilled in me the desire to fulfill His plan. In other words, the things I wanted to do were the same things that God wanted me to do. When I submitted to His will, the opportunities came rolling in.

I found myself going back to school. I found time to write books. I found time to speak at conferences across the United States. I found time to help others.

Think of the example you are setting as you step out in faith and begin to act on God's purpose in your life.

To tie this all together, is it possible that the things you want to do could have anything to do with *teaching the younger women* from Titus 2:3-5?

I believe it does. Your goals, your purpose, your desires are a perfect channel to accomplish the commandment in Titus 2:3-5.

Forty-plus women have a great deal of life experience to share with others.

Put on your *TuTu,* and get out there!

Titus 2:3-5

"Likewise, teach the older women to be reverent in the way they live, not to be slanderers or addicted to much wine, but to teach what is good. Then they can train the younger women to love their husbands and children, to be self-controlled and pure, to be busy at home, to be kind, and to be subject to their husbands, so that no one will malign the word of God." (NIV)

LF

About the Authors

Dr. Linda F. Felker

Dr. Linda F. Felker is the Owner and President of Felker Consulting, Inc. She provides professional development analysis, consultation, leadership training, authoring, and counseling. She holds a charter certification to administer the Myers Briggs Type Indicator and conducts couples, individual, and group counseling sessions on psychological and personality type in relationships.

Dr. Felker graduated *magna cum laude* from Columbia Southern University with a BSBA and a MBA in Business Management. She earned her PhD at Madison University, graduating *summa cum laude*, with studies in Human Resources and Family Counseling.

She is a frequent guest speaker at leadership and women's conferences across the country and is the author of two relationship books, *Lessons From the Purple Tree* and *Homewreckers*.

Linda and her husband David have three children, Todd, Marci, and Brent, two grandchildren, Zachary and Jackson, a daughter-in-law Ann, and two step-grandchildren, Taylor and Brooke. She is a charter member of Grace Baptist Temple.

Phyllis R. Spence

Phyllis R. Spence is the Director of the children's choir at Grace Baptist Temple in Winston-Salem, NC. She was the Founder and Director of GBT Music Camp for 11 years, taught a ladies' Bible study class, and is a member of the Adult Sanctuary Choir. Phyllis teaches private lessons in voice and piano at her music studio in Lexington, NC.

Phyllis graduated *cum laude* from Piedmont Baptist College with a Bachelor of Arts in Music. She has been a successful recording artist and a member of gospel music groups.

Phyllis is a popular guest speaker at ladies' seminars. She uses her gifts of singing and speaking to communicate and present the Gospel in a refreshing and humorous way.

Phyllis and her husband Guy have one son Brian and a daughter-in-law Jodie. She and her husband have been members of Grace Baptist Temple for over 25 years.

A Word from the Husbands

We originally asked our husbands, Guy Spence and Dave Felker, to write the **Foreword** to *Giggles in the Garden*. We could sense they were a little hesitant so we told them they could write anything they wanted to write, even if they had a story they would like to tell the readers – anything at all.

What you are about to read over the next few pages is <u>exactly</u> what they wrote for us.

We are two very blessed women.

Much love,

Phyllis and Linda

I first met Phyllis in 1967. From the beginning, I knew that she was a very unique and special individual. She had an effervescent personality and displayed an "I love life and intend to live it in its fullness" quality. To say that she was different from all the girls that I had previously known well was an understatement.

To begin with, I knew that she liked me well enough, but she would not date on the weekends; she had to sing with "her gospel quartet." I told her that I could not date except on the weekends, for I had to work. Naturally, I was the one that had to give in. Furthermore, she had eating habits that were totally foreign to me. She wouldn't eat chicken, which I thought was a universal meat. However, one Saturday morning, I had arranged to take her to work. She came out to the car with a hotdog and coke. That was her breakfast. Wow! Who was this girl that I had fallen in love with?

Now, Phyllis and I have been married for 39 years, and she still occasionally surprises me. She has always wanted more than just being a housewife. She loves working with children in church, teaching them in a youth choir. She loves exploring yard sales and auctions in order to find hidden and under-priced treasures. She is very artistic, often creating beautiful flower arrangements, etc. I can't even begin to recall how many configurations our home furniture has seen. Suffice it to say that it's not too long a period from one rearrangement to the next, even though I usually strongly resist these strenuous activities. Still, they go on.

Imagine my shock when in 1992, she told me she wanted to begin college. We had a 14-year-old son. I was nearing retirement. I figured that it was a transient phase that would quickly pass. Nevertheless, four years later, she and my son both graduated (both with honors): she from Piedmont Baptist College, he from North Davidson High School. She now holds a music degree and teaches private piano and voice lessons in her music studio. She is an excellent teacher, her students love her, and she loves them.

Some years ago, she began to receive invitations to speak at ladies' seminars and conferences. Although (quite naturally) I have never heard one of her addresses in these events, they must be pretty good and/or entertaining, for she continues to get invitations, and on a more frequent basis, I might add.

While she was taking Freshmen English at Piedmont Baptist College, she told me that her professor informed her that she should write a book, for her writing was exceptional in quality and interest. My reaction was that they should evaluate their professor, for she was probably "a few bricks shy of a load." (I suppose a treasure is most often hidden from those closest to it.) The funny thing was that many times over the previous years she had expressed a strong desire to write a book. I <u>always</u> discouraged it. Now, here we are approaching 40 years together, and she has finally completed another phase of her dreams and aspirations. She has co-authored a book. I really wonder where we go from here. Anyone care to speculate?

Phyllis, you never cease to amaze me, and I still love you! You are my best friend.

Guy Spence
July 2007

Iknew it would be a life-changing decision for me to quit my job, sell my house, and move to Winston-Salem; however, it has been much more than I imagined at the time.

I arrived in town on a Saturday and visited Grace Baptist Temple the next day. I was escorted to a Sunday School classroom, and I sat down on the second row to wait for the teacher to begin.

Just then, a beautiful, black-haired woman strolled through the door. She moved with grace and seemed to float across the floor, speaking with people, and finally selected a seat on the front row.

I was mesmerized. Sitting in front of me was the most stunning woman I had ever seen. She turned around and welcomed me to the class. Her smile just lit up her face, and her lovely eyes peered into mine. Instant Connection! I knew at that moment that I had just met the love of my life and the woman I was going to marry.

These many years later, I still get that jolt of feeling about Linda. She is a true dichotomy: 100% Lady, 100% Woman, 100% Southern Belle, all rolled into one.

I am constantly amazed at her ability to accomplish so many things at the same time. Our children and grandchildren adore her, and she makes each of them feel special and loved. Her clients admire her wisdom and insight, as she tackles problems and projects with a natural flair for success.

When she starts something, it becomes a top priority; therefore, almost everything she does is a top priority. Somehow, she manages to balance it all, and nothing or no one is ever slighted. She has accomplished remarkable things in her life, but she will tell you it is only through God's grace; she gives Him all the glory and honor.

When she decided to pursue her MBA and then PhD, she went after it with a passion. She continued to work 50–60 hours a week, took care of the home, and went to school all at the same time. Her nature is to excel, and she settles for nothing less from herself than to give her best.

She graduated with honors with her MBA and followed that by earning a PhD in Human Relations and Counseling, graduating *summa cum laude.*

She did not stop there! Next, she announced she was going to write a book. Her first book was written and published in less than six months and was a huge success in this area. Since then, she wrote another book, mentored a teenage girl while she wrote a book, taught multiple classes, facilitated conferences and seminars, and took on project after project.

I am so proud of her. Not for her accomplishments, but because of the person that she is. Through it all, her primary focus has been our family. Although she is deep into corporate activities and personal goals, our family and our church are the center of her life.

I traveled with Linda to many of her speaking engagements, everywhere from San Francisco to New York. I have watched from the back of crowded auditoriums while she mesmerized the people with her knowledge and her humor. She has a way of engaging the crowd – they love her! Yet she cuts to the heart of the topic like she is wielding a big sword! It is an amazing thing to watch.

God is her strength, and His Will is her passion. I am proud to be her husband.

I love her more today than the day we were married.

She is my heart's desire.

Dave Felker
July 2007

LaVergne, TN USA
05 March 2010
175082LV00001B/1/A